W9-BRE-037

BARBARO

BARBARO

THE HORSE WHO CAPTURED AMERICA'S HEART

BY SEAN CLANCY

EP

ECLIPSE
PRESS

Lexington, Kentucky

Library of Congress Control Number: 2007920396

ISBN: 978-1-58150-159-9

Printed in China
First Edition: 2007

a division of
Blood-Horse Publications
PUBLISHERS SINCE 1916

EP
ECLIPSE
PRESS

CONTENTS

Introduction

Michael Matz walked out of Delaware Park, muttering over a bad ride a jockey had given one of his horses. The former Olympian never gets too upset or excited about little things like rides, but this one really annoyed him.

His frustration over the ride was quickly replaced when Matz discovered a nail in a tire on his Volvo station wagon.

They say bad things come in threes, and as Matz knelt in the gravel, twisting a tire iron, his wife, DD, called. He knew something was wrong by the way she said hello.

"Barbaro foundered," DD said. "You better get to New Bolton right away."

Laminitis, the crippling and potentially fatal hoof ailment, had finally struck. Barbaro had foundered in his good foot. Six weeks after the Derby winner underwent surgery to repair his shattered right hind leg, the relative calm had come crashing down. The broken leg was fine; the once-healthy left foot was a disaster. Because of the enormous stress on it, most of the hoof wall had separated from the inner structures of the hoof.

Matz changed that tire so fast he could have been pit crew for NASCAR. Flooring it out of Delaware Park's parking lot, the trainer drove the half-hour from the racetrack to New Bolton Center in Unionville, Pennsylvania, to meet his wife; Barbaro's surgeon, Dr. Dean Richardson; and Barbaro's owners, Roy and Gretchen Jackson.

The meeting was about a horse and about what was fair for that horse.

The group tried to remain stoic, but tears flowed. By the end the only one being stoic was the horse, who stood less than ten feet away in his stall as humans decided his fate. There he was, looking at his team, just as he always did, ears up, eyes alert, head held high.

Matz looked at Barbaro and in a lifetime of making crucial decisions at crucial times, he made one more. He had the last word and made it count, imploring the Jacksons and Richardson to give the horse two weeks, give him a shot to beat this laminitis. Look, the horse hadn't lost anything in his life yet.

Everyone left New Bolton that day with a deadline. If the horse was still suffering in two weeks and the hoof looked like it wasn't healing, the game finally would be up.

The two weeks began; the clock, set. Now it was up to

Barbaro to win again. When Matz was away from New Bolton, he felt a sense of resignation that they would have to put the horse down. Then, he'd make his daily visit.

"Every time I came in, his ears were pricked over the stall door; he never showed us signs that it wasn't something he couldn't handle," Matz said. "He didn't want to die."

And so Barbaro battled on, this time facing a foe more determined, more calculating than any he had ever met on the racetrack. The undefeated horse who had captured America's heart with his flawless Kentucky Derby now had the world's attention in his greatest race yet — the race to live.

Time and again Barbaro had confounded the skeptics. Early in 2006 many in racing doubted this strapping turf specialist could transfer his talent to the dirt. Despite his unbeaten record, Derby bettors only made Barbaro the second choice. Then, when he shattered his right hind leg in the Preakness, most people expected he would be dead the next day. Few felt optimistic, either, when Barbaro endured six hours of surgery to repair his leg. Yet the colt awoke from anesthesia with a friskiness that surprised everyone.

Could Barbaro defy the odds once again?

7

"We knew he had class, and we knew he had some talent. A Derby horse?
No, nobody had any idea of that."

— BILL SANBORN

Young Promise

In November 1998 Roy and Gretchen Jackson drove up the New Jersey Turnpike to Aqueduct racetrack to see a filly named La Ville Rouge run in the grade III Tempted Stakes. The Jacksons' bloodstock adviser at the time, Kathy Rengert, thought the two-year-old filly might suit the Jacksons, who were looking to add to their racing operation.

Trained by Phil Serpe, La Ville Rouge finished second in the race, beaten a half-length by grade I winner and Phipps Stable homebred Oh What a Windfall. The Jacksons liked what they saw and bought La Ville Rouge from owners Randy Marks and Charles Balbach in hopes of enjoying her racing career and adding her to their broodmare band once her racing days ended.

Lifelong horse enthusiasts, the Jacksons had stepped up their racing and breeding interests in the late 1990s, going from dabbling with a couple of horses to attacking the sport strategically with high-end bloodlines. They were always on the lookout for quality mares to bolster their breeding platform.

Seven and a half years after that trip to Aqueduct, La Ville Rouge would become that platform's most crucial

strut, proving invaluable to the couple from West Grove, Pennsylvania.

La Ville Rouge would change their lives.

Roy Jackson's father, M. Roy Jackson, instilled the horse gene in his son. Master of the Rose Tree and Radnor hunts in Pennsylvania, he introduced the renowned Penn-Marydel breed of foxhound to America. Old-timers still talk about the rhapsodic days at Rose Tree where hunting over the post-and-rail fences turned boys to men in a matter of strides.

Roy rode as a kid but, as most boys do, turned to sports with scores instead of views. But even as he was playing shortstop and center field for his baseball team, Roy couldn't shake horses from their inherited place in his psyche. Several years after the death of his father, Jackson's mother, Almira Rockefeller, married Hardie Scott, a Philadelphia lawyer, and the couple bought a couple of mares from a dispersal of Elizabeth Arden Graham's Maine Chance Farm. Roy Jackson followed his mother and stepfather's ensuing stable, adding to his innate interest in racing.

Roy Jackson's future wife, Gretchen Schaefer, grew up in the Chestnut Hill area of Philadelphia and adored horses as a child. She grew up fox hunting, showing, and competing in hunter trials. Instead of church on Sundays, her father would take her to the Philadelphia Zoo to ride the ponies.

Roy and Gretchen Jackson met at a subscription dance series held at the Merion Tribute House during their junior year in high school but went their separate ways — for a while. Gretchen transferred from Briarcliff Junior College to the University of Pennsylvania in her sophomore year. There she reunited with Roy, now a three-sport letterman. They married in St. Thomas' Church, close to Gretchen's childhood home, in 1959. Gretchen graduated from the University of Pennsylvania that year and later earned a master's degree from Neumann College. Roy graduated in 1961 after a heart condition required surgery, derailing his sports days and delaying his graduation.

Roy Jackson tried life as a stockbroker for six years before being offered one of four intern positions for a business training program set up by former Philadelphia Phillies owner Robert Carpenter. The program also included Pat Williams, who became the executive vice president of the NBA's Orlando Magic. For a twenty-eight-year-old sports fanatic, the internship served as a golden opportunity that Jackson turned into a solid career in professional baseball. Jackson owned several minor league teams and served as president of the Eastern League, International League, and Pacific Coast League before starting his own sports agency, Convest, which represented major league ball players.

The Jacksons have four children, MacRoy, Lucy, Hardie, and Fred, and, in turn, ten grandchildren; it's been a good life, mixed with family and horses, all the way.

The Jacksons bought their first broodmare, Royal Sense, with good friend and fellow Pennsylvanian, Russell Jones, of Walnut Green Bloodstock, in the late 1970s. The couple experimented in the commercial market, selling Royal Sense's progeny at Kentucky sales and continued to search for more mares and racehorses, with modest results. It wasn't until Roy Jackson started to wind down from Convest (he sold the company in 2000) that the couple pursued the sport at a higher level.

The Jacksons had bought their first horse property near Chester Springs, Pennsylvania, naming it Lael Farm ("lael" means loyalty in Gaelic). Suburban development started to engulf Chester Springs in the early 1970s, prodding the Jacksons to move to their present farm, an idyllic 190-acre spread in the more preserved countryside surrounding Unionville, Pennsylvania, in 1978. The Jacksons named the new place — originally a dairy farm — Lael as well, and the farm has, indeed, meant loyalty to family and animals. Ponies for the grandchildren, foxhunters and racehorses long retired, not to mention miniature donkeys, sheep, dogs, and a couple of cows reside at Lael.

The farm, about forty miles southwest of Philadelphia, lies in the center of Pennsylvania horse country. Jonathan Sheppard's steeplechase spread is hacking distance down the road. Roy Jackson passes the University of Pennsylvania's New Bolton Center on his way to pick up the *Daily Racing Form* at the Landhope Farms convenience store, or as the locals call it, Willowdale. It's a place where you can buy a bagel and coffee and hire a horse trainer all at the same time.

Around Unionville, the Cheshire Foxhounds, the same

Roy and Gretchen Jackson share a lifelong love of horses

Penn-MaryDels (the best pack of hounds in Pennsylvania, now that Rose Tree is long gone) signify winter. The Jacksons' daffodils, growing along the bank of their manicured Lael Farm on Street Road, welcome spring.

Like most smaller breeders, the Jacksons board their mares in Kentucky, mostly at the historic Mill Ridge Farm, just down the road from Keeneland. La Ville Rouge leads the stellar group.

John B. Penn originally purchased La Ville Rouge, bred by Givens Farm in Florida, as a yearling for $42,000 at the Keeneland September sale. She was resold for $130,000 at the Ocala Breeders' Sales two-year-olds in training sale in March. Sent to Serpe, she won one race before finishing second in the Tempted.

The Jacksons kept La Ville Rouge with Serpe for one start, a sixth in the Demoiselle, before moving her to trainer Graham Motion and eventually to Hall of Famer P.G. Johnson.

She won six times from twenty-five starts and was graded stakes-placed on turf and on dirt while handling a route of ground. She did some of her best work going long on the grass, finishing second in the grade III Noble Damsel and third in the grade II Sheepshead Bay and Long Island handicaps, all in New York. The Jacksons retired her after her four-year-old season with $262,594 in earnings.

A daughter of the crack sprinter Carson City and Toddler Stakes winner La Reine Rouge, La Ville Rouge made a perfect broodmare for the Jacksons. She earned black type, her mother had black type, and her sire epitomized speed.

"She just missed being a really good racehorse, placing

La Ville Rouge is a cornerstone of the Jackson broodmare band

in some graded stakes but never winning one," Roy Jackson said. "When it came time to breed her, she is kind of narrow, and we were trying to get more bone."

More bone, they got. With help from Headley Bell's Nicoma Bloodstock, the Jacksons selected Saint Ballado for La Ville Rouge's first mating and Dynaformer for her second. Dynaformer had climbed a long ladder in the breeding world, going from a $5,000 stud fee when he started in 1990 to a $50,000 stud fee by the time the Jacksons decided to send La Ville Rouge to Three Chimneys Farm near Lexington to the son of Roberto (Dynaformer now stands for $150,000). Known best for producing high-class turf performers, Dynaformer has never been fashionable for the sales market, just proven and potent for the racing side. His progeny show over and over that tough, solid, durable racehorses can make a man a lot of money.

La Ville Rouge's first foal, named Holy Ground, hit the ground tall and robust. Her second came from the same mold, massive at birth. His name, Barbaro.

The strapping bay colt would have fit right in around the Jacksons' hometown, where folks love their horses. Especially a well-made, beautifully bred statue of a horse that could lead a steeplechase schooling set in Sheppard's Hall of Fame operation or lead the hunt field over the renowned Brooklawn Double, a set of post-and-rail fences on either side of a country road not far from the Jacksons' farm.

Bill Sanborn foaled Barbaro at Springmint Farm, a 257-acre farm near Nicholasville, Kentucky, that he and his wife, Sandy, leased for their breeding operation, Sanborn Chase. A thirty-year veteran of foaling mares, Sanborn had boarded the Jacksons' mares since 1994. He was there for La Ville Rouge's

first foaling, when Holy Ground had to be pulled out because of his size. Knowing that Dynaformer tends to produce big foals too, Sanborn was ready on the night of April 29, 2003, when La Ville Rouge began to show signs of distress.

When they saw two white hooves poking out, Sanborn and his night watchman, Irvin White, gently pulled a big bay colt into this world.

The wet and wide-eyed colt tried to stand up in the foaling stall. Barbaro's long legs couldn't quite get it together, and the young foal struggled to discover his balance.

"Barbaro was similar to his brother, as far as size-wise," Sanborn recalled. "It took him a while to get himself together because he was so big."

Both Holy Ground and Barbaro get their size from the paternal sides. They get their temperament from their mother, an easy-going mare who caused little notice around Sanborn Chase. Her first two foals inherited her docile nature.

Holy Ground lazily went through the motions at Sanborn Chase. He'd be the last horse to gallop in from the field and the first one to fall asleep in the barn. Keith Richie was in charge of familiarizing the babies to routine care. Nicknamed Seemore (his seven brothers said the more he saw, the more he ate), Richie loved Holy Ground and would crawl into his stall and rest his head on the colt's belly.

Barbaro wasn't as laid back as Holy Ground, but he made friends quicker than the first kid to get a car in high school. Named after a foxhound in a treasured painting that hangs in the Jacksons' home, Barbaro hit it off with Sanborn.

"Both of them were as nice a horse as you'd want to be

Dynaformer has excelled as a sire of sturdy turf horses

around," Sanborn said. "The first foal would sleep all the time. Literally, you'd bring him in, he'd eat, lie down, and sleep, and you had to wake him up to eat before he went out. Barbaro wasn't that laid back, but he never had an evil temperament; he was just the sweetest thing."

As a weanling, Barbaro came in from the field with a splint, a minor calcium lump on a horse's splint bone, which runs next to the cannon bone in the front legs, and needed stall rest for a couple of weeks. Locked up in the stall where he was born, Barbaro became day and night watchman, analyzing everything and everyone from his stall.

"He could just get his nose out over the stall door, and he liked that," Sanborn said. "He was like an old track horse, just hung his head out and looked at stuff. He loved to look at stuff. He never got rank in the stall; he was a perfect patient."

Every time Sanborn walked by the colt's stall, he'd scratch his muzzle and talk to the colt he called "La Ville." Life on a breeding farm is funny — Sanborn called Holy Ground "La Ville" too. And the third foal, Man in Havana, yup, he also went by "La Ville." Sanborn was around three different La Villes, but there was only one Barbaro.

"Hey, La Ville, what's happening, how you feeling this morning?" Sanborn would say to the colt and then pat him on his head. La Ville, er, Barbaro would look at Sanborn, curious as a kitten. In a barn with constant activity, Barbaro demanded attention, just by hanging his head over his stall door and pleading for it. He coaxed a pat from anyone who walked past, just a touch on the big white splotch between his eyes. He loved the attention.

Barbaro was one of about ten other yearlings that Sanborn

raised in 2004. They say Thoroughbreds need to run in packs as young horses; the early days of play hone their competitive nature and prime them to be racehorses. Barbaro didn't need much class work in that department.

"This colt never held back," Sanborn said. "Holy Ground would hold back and then barge through the rest of the horses, once they got to the gate. Barbaro had a much more forward mind, more of a race mind. We knew he had class,

and we knew he had some talent. A Derby horse? No, nobody had any idea of that."

One thing was for sure, La Ville Rouge threw two impressive foals in her first two tries.

"Looking at the first two foals, there was something special about her," Sanborn said. "I knew that she could be a real serious broodmare and [the Jacksons] saw it too. It was a no brainer. She just put a big, strong foal on the ground.

She was the kind of broodmare you want to keep."

In November it was time for Sanborn to pack up Barbaro for a trip to John and Jill Stephens' training center in Ocala, Florida, where the next stage of his education would begin.

Barbaro arrived at the 110-acre spread in early fall, one of sixty yearlings to enter the Stephens' kindergarten class. Here Barbaro and his classmates would learn to accept the bit, the bridle, then the saddle and rider. Learn to steer, to jog under tack, carry a rider, listen to a rider, get used to having a job for the first time in their lives. By spring, they'd be breezing slowly and ready to go to the racetrack.

John Stephens would like to tell you that he knew Barbaro was a future Derby winner when the yearling stepped off the van from Sanborn Chase. But that would be a lie. What he did know was that the raw colt showed off a big, long leg and some presence.

"Just a leggy Dynaformer colt, he had some scope and size to him, but he was just a horse," Stephens said. "He had the frame for it, but it's like a six-foot-seven man; when they're a kid, they don't look the same."

John and and his wife tried to build one thing when they began Stephens Training Center in 1999: a horse-friendly environment. With a three-quarters-mile training track and lots of trees and paddocks, the couple developed a facility where they could let horses be horses.

Horses can be ridden on the trails, in the field, or on the racetrack. Nothing's pushed but wheelbarrows around the Stephens' operation. Horses have a job to do, but at this stage in their lives, they tell the trainer what they're ready for and when they're ready for it.

John Stephens grew up in Arizona and learned horses

Bill Sanborn, shown opposite with his wife Sandy, helped deliver Barbaro, pictured above as a foal

the proper way — starting with an after-school job mucking stalls. At sixteen, he bought a pickup truck and needed to pay for it. Mucking stalls paid cash, and it beat bagging groceries. When his boss was ruled off the racetrack, Stephens applied for a trainer's license. Eighteen years old and training horses, Stephens bounced around with some cheap horses from Turf Paradise to Penn National, eventually working for a veterinary practice in New Jersey.

"I was just trying to learn how to be a good horseman because I didn't grow up with horses," Stephens said.

Stephens became a good enough horseman to start his own breaking and training operation in Ocala. The Stephenses have built up a steady line of clients including New York-based trainer Christophe Clement who introduced the couple to the Jacksons.

Barbaro spent a couple of easy weeks before Jill Stephens hooked up a set of long draw reins and began walking behind him, steering him with the long reins to form the base of his education. Barbaro and Stephens covered the farm, turning right, then left, then stopping, then moving forward, turning in figure-eights, circles, off in a straight line.

Once content with the colt's progress, Jill climbed aboard Barbaro and gradually put him through the paces of racehorse education 101. First, field work, where the horses walk and jog in circles, then figure eights before loping in both directions.

"Just riding so they want to be ridden," John Stephens said. "It doesn't matter what kind of discipline you're doing, just basic horsemanship stuff."

Barbaro spent about thirty days getting the hang of a rider before seeing the training track for the first time.

"He was always a nice horse. Things were always very easy for him, and he was always a very intelligent horse," Stephens said. "He did everything the right way, and the reports were given to Mr. and Mrs. Jackson that he was showing to be a nice horse. But being a nice horse at the farm and being a good racehorse are two totally different things."

Stephens Training Center, operated by John and Jill Stephens, gives future racehorses their early lessons

Not that Stephens tested Barbaro for anything more than cooperation for the job at hand. Doing a good job on the farm means systematic education where horses learn to like their work.

"People will say, 'how didn't you know right away?' " Stephens said. "Well, when you're doing a good job at the farm, you're not pushing them that hard. The farm is just

John Stephens and Barbaro's half brother, Man in Havana

education; he was just here learning his ABCs. But, in doing that, he learned the ABCs faster than anyone else. And he always looked for more."

Barbaro was already a big, strong horse and a good-feeling horse, but he managed himself with class. His mind was there from the start, the one that could process the information, get the concept, and go about doing what was asked without losing a beat. He was breezing three furlongs with ease by the time spring came around.

"You're really not asking for their lives here at the farm. You're just making sure they respond, that they're professional, that they'll take dirt in their face, that they can breeze in company without shying away," Stephens said. "You're just not asking them for that extra gear here. I don't care if it's jumpers, racehorses, cutting horses; you see horses that just make it look easier than other horses, and that's always been his thing. He made things look pretty easy."

Through years of disappointment, Stephens has learned to temper his excitement about young horses that shine in their early lessons. Sure, file it away, but don't get carried away; this is pre-school in a lifetime of education.

"You keep your fingers crossed, and you hope they all make it to whatever level they are," Stephens said. "They're like human athletes; they all have their limits whatever that is. Hell, you're happy to have any kind of stakes horse much less a grade I horse."

As at any other school, some pupils pick up the lessons quickly and some never get them completely. Breaking babies is about doing the best you can with what you have and sending future racehorses on their way with, hopefully, enough education and groundwork that they'll reach their potential. Favorites? Of course there are favorites, even if the teacher isn't supposed to admit it.

La Ville Rouge was proving to be a favorite mother. Stephens taught Holy Ground, who went through the same program and gave a positive impression while picking up the basics of being a racehorse.

"He was a different type of horse. Holy Ground was a little bit stronger-looking horse, a faster-looking horse. He was all business, but things were always easier for Barbaro," Stephens said. "Holy Ground, we knew was a nice horse when he left, but Barbaro you just didn't see any limit on him. I say that, listen, we didn't know he was going to be a grade I horse or a Derby winner, but we saw a lot of positives."

The Jacksons visited Barbaro early in 2005 and immediately knew what Stephens was talking about.

"He was really starting to change and mature into a nice horse, but you never know," Roy Jackson said. "We've been in this for a long time, and you have some that are terrific physically but don't have heart."

Thoroughbreds will make realists out of the starriest dreamers. After a lifetime of learning hard lessons about horses, Stephens knew Barbaro was different than most of the other horses he sends to trainers, but he also knew Barbaro was finishing the easiest part of his racing life and a mountain awaited.

"Sometimes the worst thing you can do is have a horse too long. They're all time bombs; it's just that their clocks are set different. Sooner or later something's going to go wrong. Most of them, it's sooner," Stephens said. "Some of them you can't help, and some of them help you. You could put some of them in a rubber stall and they'd have a rubber allergy and die on you."

That's why Stephens was happy to send Barbaro on his way — diploma signed, sealed, and delivered — to Fair Hill Training Center. To the waiting hands of Michael Matz.

Reluctant Hero

Michael Matz is not your typical horse trainer. He's a purist, a horseman first, the type of guy who likes to train horses and be around horses in the morning as much as he likes to run them. Not that he doesn't run them. He runs them often and they win often. He just likes horses, more for who they are than what they can do for him.

In Matz' nearly forty-year career, accomplished horses — from Hall of Fame show jumper Jet Run to grade I stakes winner Kicken Kris — hold a special spot in his heart. Equally singed in his mind are the ones he thinks he betrayed. The ones he thinks he let down.

In 2002, two years after officially retiring from a glorious show-jumping career and just six years into his fledgling Thoroughbred training career, Matz conditioned a horse named Saint Marden, a decent colt by Saint Ballado. The chestnut colt had talent, good enough to win the grade III Discovery Handicap in the fall of his three-year-old year. After the Discovery, Saint Marden started to bleed in every breeze leading up to his next goal, the lucrative Sunshine Millions program in early 2003. Matz anguished over how to alleviate the problem but just couldn't stop the horse from bleeding. He breezed; he bled. Finally, Matz told the owner the horse needed time.

The owner told Matz he was a businessman and was willing to take a gamble. Matz, with reservation, saddled Saint Marden in the Sunshine Millions, knowing he was sending a boy to do a man's job. In his eighth career start, Saint Marden bled, finished last, and never raced again.

"I knew I didn't have the horse fit enough because I couldn't. He never ran another race in his life," Matz said. "I felt sad for that horse. He had a lot of ability, and I just plain ruined that horse. I'm lucky I just don't have any people like that any more. And I'm not taking any either because it just doesn't work.

Matz concedes that it costs him more in terms of staff to provide his horses with the best care. "But I feel safe, and I'd rather get it done the right way than scrimp, because the one that gets hurt is the horse," he said.

Around Matz' stable, divided among two barns at Fair Hill, one at Delaware Park, and his farm in Unionville, Pennsylvania, it's easy to see Matz' philosophy at work. Loyal owners send potent stock, which receive the best care possible. No nonsense. No fluff. Every action has a purpose.

"I like the standard in the barn to be high. I like the horses to look well, everything to be done the right way," Matz said. "I like things done in a certain way, and I like things done in the right way. I don't like loose ends. If I was a customer and I came into the barn and everything is in shambles, I would say, 'Jeez, if he takes care of this, this way, then how is he taking care of my horse?' That's just plain common courtesy to the customer."

Matz will fret over a noseband that's too low on a horse's head, and when a filly comes up lame on the day of a stakes, with the owners already in the air, he's frustrated but buckets are not kicked. Matz is soft-spoken, courteous, poised, and, above all, professional.

Matz' office at Fair Hill looks more like a lobby of a law firm than a barn office. (Matz kept his show stable name, Vintage Farm, for his racing stable.) And Matz himself shows the same care with his own appearance. His hair is neatly combed, his boots are polished, and he keeps himself as fit as when he was riding for a living. In the mornings, dressed in mahogany-colored chaps and velvet hunt cap and astride his track pony, Matz is the picture of the polished equestrian. In the afternoons, Matz arrives at the track meticulously groomed in a dark blazer, tailored shirt, and tasteful tie or on big race days, a conservative suit that would pass at any boardroom around the world.

Born January 23, 1951, in Reading, Pennsylvania, Matz grew up with his two younger brothers in a three-bedroom house in the small town of Shillington, a suburb of Reading, the northernmost point of a triangle formed by Philadelphia and Lancaster, in eastern Pennsylvania.

The son of a plumber, Matz didn't ride his first horse until his early teens. He was too busy helping his father. The elder Matz paid his son and a friend forty dollars a week to backfill sewers. It was back-breaking work, but Michael said he felt like a rock star when he got his cash at the end of the week.

"Now, I think about what it would have cost him, son of a gun, to hire a back hoe to fill those things in an hour, he got two guys for all week," Matz recalled with a chuckle. "It probably kept us out of trouble."

On weekends Matz' father got him a job on a friend's farm, doing odd chores. Matz was earning an hourly wage and staying out of trouble when farm owner George Kohl changed his life with a simple question.

"Do you know how to ride?" Kohl asked Matz.

"Oh sure," Matz lied.

Kohl had just bought two horses, a four-year-old for himself and a fourteen-year-old for his wife. Kohl's wife wasn't interested in riding so Matz became the deputy. The teenager had never been on a horse and did it to keep his job.

Matz rode the older horse around the farm, basically doing nothing more than hanging onto the martingale as the horse followed his stablemate — walk, jog, canter — Matz didn't know the difference. This wasn't equitation; it was horseback riding where the horse makes the decision and the rider hangs on until it's over. One day Kohl couldn't ride the four-year-old and asked Matz to give him some light exercise around the farm.

Like what usually happens when a green rider and a green horse collide — the walk became a jog, the jog became a canter, the canter became a hell-bent hundred-yard dash

Matz earned a bronze medal at the Pan Am Games in 1975

back to the barn.

"The son of a gun ran right into the stable, and there was the tractor and manure spreader; he stopped right in front of the tractor and I flew over it," Matz recalled. "I said, 'That's enough for me.' Right then, the guy walked out and said, 'Come on, you've got to get right back on.' I said, 'Nah, I've had enough of this stuff.'"

Nevertheless, Matz did climb back aboard that horse and liked riding enough to join the local Berks Pony Club, where he began to learn the basics of horsemanship and feel the first tinge of a competitiveness that would serve him throughout his life.

Like in most pony clubs, boys were scarce, but the ones that did participate became fast friends. Matz hit it off with Scott Palmer, who went to the neighboring high school in Wyomissing. Matz and Palmer went to every horse show or pony club rally available.

Nearing the end of their high school days, the two teenage buddies contemplated life after high school while waiting their turn to compete at a horse show in Pennsylvania.

It was 1968 — Bobby Kennedy, Martin Luther King Jr., the Vietnam War. Sex, drugs, and rock n' roll. Rebellion was in.

"Scott, what do you want to do when you get out of school?" Matz asked his friend.

"I'm not sure," Palmer said. "I might want to go to college and go to law school. What about you?"

"I'm thinking I want to try to make a go at the horse business," Matz said.

"I don't know how you're going to make a living with

Winning the 1981 FEI Jumping World Cup Final aboard Jet Run

horses. Can you really do that?" Palmer asked.

"Just watch," Matz told him.

Matz failed the physical when drafted number 48 for the Vietnam War (his left arm bows out like a busted guitar string). He signed up for two classes at Albright College, a satellite program to Penn State, but school suffocated him. He wanted to be a show rider and itched to learn more and make up for his horseless childhood. Competitive by nature, Matz wanted to jump horses, a sport in which time and precision mean everything. In his mind, time was a-wasting. He wanted to be out there competing against Bill Steinkraus and 1968 Olympic gold medal winner Snowbound.

Ironically, Palmer would go on to make his living in the horse business, too, scrapping law school for veterinary school and eventually becoming director and chief surgeon of the New Jersey Equine Clinic in Clarksburg, a couple of hours from Matz' home base at Fair Hill.

Matz' first move once he decided that horses would be his thing was to get a job with well-known show rider Bernie Traurig.

At Traurig's farm, Matz started the day with a feeding chart and a feed cart full of oats. With upward of sixty horses to look after, Matz spent all morning feeding, haying, and watering. By the time that was done, it was almost noon, and he'd start doling out lunch, which would quickly turn into dinnertime when he'd start the whole process over. Matz wasn't an hourly wage kid looking to pick up a few dollars for a Friday night out; no, Matz was studying Traurig's horses. This one in the corner cleaned up six quarts; the one out back won't touch his hay; the new filly hasn't cleaned up since she's been here. Matz might have hated school, but he

was a natural student. He processed everything there was to know about horses and learned the basics of horse care.

Matz left Traurig and got a job with Vince Dugan in West Chester, Pennsylvania. Dugan's stable, across the street from the University of Pennsylvania's equine hospital, New Bolton Center, is known for wheeling and dealing a lot of horses. It was a perfect spot for an ambitious kid to develop his riding. Matz stayed at Dugan's for several years, riding sale horses as if he were test-driving cars. Racehorse people finish work in the morning so they can get to the races in the afternoon. Show horse people think, why rush, what are you going to do with the rest of your day? Matz spent all day peppering young horses with jump combinations, warming up owners' horses for the weekend shows, and learning the nuances of riding show horses.

Matz then took a job riding for J. Basil Ward in Ohio, furthering his education. When Ward retired from the business, Matz got his first big break — or made his first big break — when he began riding for F. Eugene and Edie Dixon. A sportsman and philanthropist, Dixon owned a farm in Lafayette, Pennsylvania, and would become an extraordinary patron to Matz. The two men shared a dedication to hard work and gained a mutual respect that led to friendship and loyalty that far outlasted their very first business relationship. Dixon was loyal to the core.

Seven years after doing an aerial over the manure spreader, Matz made the American show-jumping team. Three years after that, he competed in the Montreal Olympics in 1976. At twenty-five, he learned his most valuable lesson — one he would carry from showing to racing.

Aboard Rhum IV at the 1996 Olympics and carrying the U.S. flag in the games' closing ceremony

Matz and his mount Grande racked up a disastrous twenty-eight faults in their round. To make things worse, the American team of Frank Chapot, Robert Ridland, William Brown, and Matz finished fourth, a point out of the medals.

"I didn't have any horse left; I had twenty-eight faults, seven poles down," Matz said. "I remember sitting there after my round, watching the teleprompter, and all I could think about was the thrill of victory and agony of defeat. None of my teammates came up to me; jeesh, I guess you learn from your mistakes. I ran out of horse."

This lesson would stick with Matz. Up until then Matz failed to understand the importance of having a fresh horse. His Olympic horse was talented enough; he was just worn out from training and preliminary rounds. Matz had pressed Grande to get to the dance; once there, though, the horse was too tired to pick up his feet. The lesson? Sometimes it's more about finding the balance between freshness and fitness.

It was a long drive back from Canada. Matz knew he had made a mistake in Montreal and vowed not to do it again. Listen to your horse; these aren't cars where you can put your foot on the gas for as long as needed. The 1976 Olympics, in front of the world, is a hard place to learn that lesson.

At those same Olympics, eight-year-old Thoroughbred gelding Jet Run finished twenty-first under Mexican rider Fernando Senderos. The Maryland-bred had won the New York Grand Prix at age six. Sold to Mexico, Jet Run took the individual gold and team silver in the 1975 Pan American Games under Senderos, before his effort in the Olympics. (Matz had earned a bronze medal at the Pan Am Games.)

After the Olympics, Dixon purchased Jet Run and returned him to the United States for Matz to ride. Matz and Jet Run soared to the top of the sport. When Jet Run sensed pressure, he jumped higher and went quicker. Matz and Jet Run won the gold medal (team and individual) at the 1979 Pan American Games in Puerto Rico. The United States boycott of the 1980 Summer Olympics quite possibly deprived Matz and Jet Run of their finest hour. In 1981 Matz and Jet Run won the FEI Jumping World Cup Final in England on the way to the American Grandprix Association Horse of the Year title for Jet Run. Both Jet Run and Michael Matz would eventually be inducted into the Show Jumping Hall of Fame.

Matz performed beautifully on a horse; young kids wanted to ride like him. Precision and finesse in the ring and the quintessential taskmaster at home, Matz won the American Grandprix Association's Rider of the Year in 1981 and again in 1984.

Matz had, indeed, succeeded in the horse business. He traveled around the world, made decent money, and was about to marry DD Alexander, an accomplished equestrian in her own right and a granddaughter of Robert Kleberg of the King Ranch, when everything he knew was tested.

On July 19, 1989, Matz and Alexander were flying home to Philadelphia after judging a horse show in Hawaii. They missed their connection in Denver and had a choice between two flights, twenty minutes apart.

Matz and Alexander boarded United Flight 232 from Denver to Philadelphia, via Chicago. The flight was near capacity with just five vacant seats. Because of their late booking, the couple sat in different sections of the plane, Matz finding himself surrounded by three unaccompanied siblings, who were flying to see their grandmother in Albany, New York.

About an hour into the two-hour flight, as the plane flew above Iowa at about 33,000 feet and began a gentle right turn to head directly to Chicago, the Douglas DC-10's number two engine failed. Passengers heard a loud explosion from the back of the plane and the aircraft shuddered. A flight attendant was knocked to the floor.

The flight deck announced that an engine had failed, and the plane would be a little late arriving in Chicago. Blowing an engine is not ideal, but any of the three engines are designed to power the plane, alone, in an emergency. But the explosion of engine number two had sent a 370-pound titanium disk into the plane's three hydraulic systems, severing them.

When Captain Al Haynes, first officer William Records, and flight engineer Dudley Dvorak discovered that the aircraft's hydraulic system had failed — rendering the aircraft basically uncontrollable — they notified controllers at Minneapolis-St. Paul Airport.

One minute after the explosion, Haynes, a thirty-three-year United Airlines veteran, relayed that the plane had developed "complete hydraulic failure." The controller initially instructed Haynes to head to Dubuque, Iowa, about 240 miles away, but the plane continued to flutter like a wounded bird so controllers directed it to the closest airport, in Sioux City, seventy miles away. The Sioux City airport, on the east bank of the Missouri River, had a runway of about 9,000 feet, long enough to land the DC-10. It also had a 7,000-foot and a 6,600-foot runway.

The aircraft continued to roll from side to side, motivating an off-duty United pilot, Dennis Fitch, who was on his way home from instructing a flight school in Denver, to the front of the plane to help his colleagues. Fitch, who had ample experience flying the DC-10, got down on his knees in the cockpit and tried to direct the throttles manually. The plane could only make wide right turns, and the officers tried to control the plane by alternating engine thrust, accelerating and decelerating the right and left engines. In pilot speak, it's called "porpoising." In reality, it's pure desperation.

Haynes got back on the intercom and warned the passengers.

"We're going to make an emergency landing in Sioux City," Haynes said. "It's going to be rough. As a matter of fact, it's going to be more than rough."

Matz played cards, trying to distract nine-year-old Travis and twelve-year-old Melissa Roth — and himself — while fourteen-year-old Jody Roth sat next to the window, a few rows ahead.

The Sioux City tower called local police and rescue units to the airport. Meanwhile, the aircraft's crew dumped fuel and lowered the landing gear in preparation for the crash landing. The airplane continued to turn right, the pilots unable to alter airspeed and the rate of descent. As the plane plummeted through the sky, Matz vowed to get the three children to safety.

At 3:53, a voice on the intercom startled passengers with a three-word instruction.

"Brace! Brace! Brace!"

Passengers put their heads down and grabbed their ankles. Four minutes later, with basically no ability to slow the plane down, Haynes was unable to line up for runway thirty-one (on a northwest bearing of 310 degrees) where emergency crews were waiting. Without a choice, he aimed as best he could at runway 22 (southwest at 220 degrees) and arrived there unbelievably steady for a plane without any hydraulic controls.

"I think I'm going to make it," Haynes radioed the tower. Almost.

The plane's right wing dipped and slammed into the ground first, just short of the runway, sending the plane nose-diving into the ground like a dart. The plane then flipped twice before landing upside down in a rain-soaked cornfield. The aircraft shattered into pieces as fire, smoke, and debris collided into a bloom of chaos.

The nose, the flight deck, and the passenger area that had been attached to the wings were the only parts of the plane left intact. Miraculously, as the rescue crew emerged on the scene, passengers began stepping out of the debris. Matz never lost sight of the Roth children despite the desperateness of the situation. Matz instructed Travis and Melissa to grab his belt and Jody to follow him out of the debris. Once clear, Matz told them to run, not to look back, just run. Matz then returned to the plane to look for DD, and when he heard cries from a baby, he and another passenger helped rescue an eleven-month-old girl out of the luggage compartment.

Matz escaped from the burning hulk and about forty minutes later, found DD safe and sound at a Red Cross station, talking to the Roth children. DD and Michael then stayed with the children for the next twenty-four hours until they were reunited with their parents.

Seat assignment ultimately decided lives. Nearly every passenger in the thirty-two-seat first-class section died, while almost all of the 117 passengers in the economy class directly behind them lived. In all, 184 passengers survived, as did seven out of eight crew members while 109 passengers died.

It was the tenth deadliest airplane crash in American flight history.

Matz was voted ABC's person of the week for his heroism.

"You just do what comes naturally to you," Matz said, matter of factly. "If the same thing happened to my children, I would want someone to do the same."

While some survivors wrote books about the crash, sued United Airlines, or went on motivational speaking engagements, the Matzes married and tried to get on with their lives. DD and Michael would rarely talk about it. Years later Michael came across a television over-dramatization that depicted the crash.

"You never know what somebody else's perspective is on something like that. The guy next to me had no idea of getting the kids out; I had to push him out of his seat. Then, there he is narrating the show, 'We did this; we did that,' " Matz said. "He used to call me, until one year when he called and asked me if I was going to the reunion, I said, 'No, I'm not flying out there.' Then I said, 'Look, if it helps you to talk to me, I'm willing to do it, but I'm not making a big deal out of this. I put it behind my life and forgot about it.' I never heard from him again."

Two weeks after the crash Matz was competing as if nothing had happened. Jet Run had been retired, but new mount Heisman picked up right where Jet Run had left off. Owned by WGHR Farm and Sale Johnson, Heisman completed six out of seven clear Olympic Trials to give Matz his second shot at the Olympics. In the 1992 Barcelona games, the team of Matz, his student Lisa Jacquin, Norman Dello Joio, and Anne Kursinski finished fifth.

Along with riding at the top level, show riders usually

Matz with Arlington Park president Richard L. Duchossois and wife DD after Kicken Kris' victory in the 2004 Arlington Million

teach a gaggle of students, going on the road to shows with horses of every level. Matz taught everyone from amateur owners wanting to survive eight jumps in the hunter ring to up-and-coming riders wanting to be the next Michael Matz. His wife was a top-notch show rider herself. He held his students, just like he held his horses, to the same standard he set for himself. Matz was patient with his horses, rarely over-stepping their abilities. He could ride any type of horse and developed most of his top horses himself.

Matz returned to the Olympics in Atlanta in 1996 riding the Dixons' Rhum IV. Through a deluge of rain, Rhum knocked down a rail in his first round and then put a foot in the liverpool to add another four faults in the second round. The German team wrested the gold from the American team of Matz, Peter Leone, Leslie Burr-Howard, and Anne Kursinski.

After earning the team silver medal, Matz received the honor of carrying the American flag at the closing ceremonies. The honor was bestowed upon him by the captains of the other American teams competing in the Olympics, a true testament to Matz' character. They voted for Michael Matz over Carl Lewis and other better-known athletes.

His fellow Olympians chose him to carry the flag, not because he talked about rescuing children from the burning wreckage of a plane but because he didn't talk about it unless asked or, more likely, prodded. Matz learned to deflect the attention to other parts of his life — mostly riding.

After the Atlanta Olympics, forty-five at the time and the sport's leading money-winning rider, Matz started to realize it was time to think about other directions.

Matz had plenty of students who wanted lessons. He could have given clinics, flown around the world judging shows or designing courses; none of that charged his psyche. So began his metamorphosis from show jump rider to racehorse trainer. He was always intrigued by racing and he's a competitor at heart, so racing seemed like a logical fit. DD's family is immersed in it, and Matz had other clients and contacts from his showing days with the same crossover interest.

Michael and DD had started a family (they now have four kids from their marriage) and Matz looked back at what he missed when raising his two children from an early marriage and decided he wasn't going to do that again. Matz searched for his next move. He didn't mind teaching, but he knew he didn't want to stand in a ring all day giving riding

Matz sweats over the details: "I like the standard in the barn to be high."

lessons. He knew he could train show horses, but riding other people's horses all day looked like pure boredom to Matz. He knew he needed a challenge just like he had needed throughout his whole life.

Two years after the Atlanta Games, Matz took out his trainer's license while fulfilling a commitment to try and get to the 2000 Olympics. He failed to make the team while splitting his time between a do-it-yourself racing stable at Delaware

Park and a waning show stable at his farm in Collegeville, Pennsylvania. After missing the 2000 Olympics, Matz put away his red coat and became a full-time horse trainer.

"I just felt like [racing] was something I could do," Matz said. "I knew I was going from the top of one thing to the bottom of another, but I always liked the racehorses and it was a challenge."

Show riders aren't simply jockeys, doing a job for two minutes. They're trainers who on the day of the competition become jockeys. Michael Matz was the Jerry Bailey of show jumping — and the Bill Mott. Training the horse comes first. Show riders recruit their owners and then need to communicate with them, placate them, and understand them. Matz attracted top owners with his thorough, exacting nature of making and competing horses.

It's the person who can master the dichotomy of caretaker and competitor who wins the most. Matz has been training horses in one form or another his whole life.

Matz began with three horses at Delaware Park. DD grabbed an exercise saddle and a rub rag, and the couple started the climb. Matz, as he did in show jumping, figured he'd outwork the rest of them and take it from there.

"My feeling is, with anything, you get out of things what you put into them. I wasn't the most talented rider, but I worked at it. I might not be the best trainer, but I'll work at it to make sure it works," Matz said. "I've been lucky to have good people to work around and to have good owners that give me the chance, whether in show jumping or here, they trust that I'll be fair and give them 125 percent. You need that backing to give you that confidence to go on."

Matz followed other notable equestrians such as Jim Day, Rodney Jenkins, Roger Attfield, and Tim Ritchey into Thoroughbred racing. As they'd tell you, a good horse is a good horse.

Barbaro's half brother Holy Ground

Matz and his star pupil, Barbaro

"Even when I showed, during the week you could go in as many preliminary classes as you wanted, but nobody cared who won the preliminary classes. They only cared who won Sunday afternoon in the grand prix," Matz said. "In racing, it's always nice to win a race whether it's a $5,000 claimer or not, but I want it to be Saturday afternoon. When I first started, I said, I've got to find a way to be there on Saturday afternoon, not Monday, Tuesday, Wednesday, Thursday, Friday afternoon, but Saturday afternoon."

Matz won his first stakes, just two years into his training career when his wife's Camella won the Silver Spoon Stakes at Delaware Park. The filly went on to win three more stakes in 2000, helping Matz gain some attention for his new endeavor.

Dixon and his wife, Edie, simply switched their support for Matz from the show-jumping arena to the racing oval and campaigned stakes horses such as Political Attack, Only in Philly, and Aunt Henny with Matz. Fellow Pennsylvanian Betty Moran sent Kicken Kris, who went on to win the 2003 Secretariat Stakes at Arlington to provide Matz with his first grade I victory. He returned a year later to win the 2004 Arlington Million.

After observing Matz' horsemanship in the show ring, Roy and Gretchen Jackson, of nearby Lael Stables in West Grove, Pennsylvania, joined Matz' burgeoning operation. They sent him La Ville Rouge's first foal, Holy Ground, who would win a minor stakes at Delaware Park, and her second foal, Barbaro, who would rock the world.

Latent Talent

The heralded Barbaro arrived at Michael Matz' barn at Fair Hill in April 2005. The growing colt, who had done nothing more on the racetrack than breeze three furlongs, had already earned his fair share of attention in Ocala. Good horses pick up fans, and Barbaro had collected a following before he left Florida.

Some of it was based on his older half brother, Holy Ground. Some of it came from the way he moved; some of it induced by the way he looked. Whether it was Bill Sanborn or John Stephens or the Jacksons or just backstretch chatter between a couple of exercise riders, Barbaro arrived in Fair Hill with a positive scouting report.

Holy Ground's half brother, big, long-striding colt, natural mover, no problems, easy way about everything. Wait until you see him.

Trainers try to ignore hype on horses that show up in their barn, choosing to form their own opinions instead. It was obvious to Matz — and to anyone else — that Barbaro had an impressive body and a decent stride; the rest would unfold with time.

"Everybody had high expectations," Matz said. "Everybody said, 'Wait until you see the Dynaformer colt that's a half to Holy Ground.'"

Matz handed the raw, unfinished colt to Peter Brette, who had begun working for Matz that spring. A retired jockey who still looked ready to ride a race, Brette was immediately impressed with Barbaro.

Ride a horse around a shed row one time and you'll get a feeling of what kind of horse you're on. No, you can't say it's a Derby winner, but you can tell enough to know if you want to go for a gallop. Little things like whether the horse possesses natural balance, innate coordination, pliable demeanor, a positive attitude. The more good horses you ride, the quicker you'll recognize the next one. Whether Barbaro could stay sound or if he'd have enough heart for the job or if he could translate any of his morning traits to the afternoon still remained to be seen, and Brette, for one, knew he wanted to find out.

Born in Stockton-on-Tees in England, Brette left home at sixteen to gallop horses in Newmarket, Britain's premier training center. Newmarket serves as college for wannabe jockeys who show up in droves trying to become the next

Lester Piggott. Brette struggled to make it as a jockey and eventually landed a break when he spent four months in Dubai, where proper Thoroughbred racing was just beginning to take hold. Brette enjoyed his time in Dubai but returned to England where his career continued to struggle mightily. Though he always looked stylish on a horse, Brette couldn't latch onto a steady stream of competitive horses. Brette met trainer Bill Mather, who offered him a job as assistant trainer and stable jockey in Dubai. There wasn't much to stay home for, so Brette packed his tack bag and went back to Dubai for a steady paycheck and perhaps a shot to ride nice horses.

"This was about twenty years ago, and there wasn't much racing over there," Brette said recently. "I remember when the Nad al Sheba grandstand was just a hole in the ground. Bill offered me a two-year contract, and I figured I had nothing to lose and could always go back to England if it didn't work out."

Brette never had to limp back to England. In 1991 the opening of Jebel Ali Racecourse in Dubai gave Brette a golden first step into a successful career.

"Everything snowballed from there," Brette said. "Sheikh Mohammed became interested in me, and by the end of the season, I was champion jockey. Things began falling into place, and we were competitive for the next ten years. Then, all of a sudden, we weren't competitive any longer. Bill retired in 2000, and things were changing rapidly in Dubai. I had a choice to stay and ride or try to get a job as a trainer."

Brette opened a stable in Dubai but struggled and knew he needed to look for other opportunities. With a wife and a young son to support, Brette decided to try America. He took a job running the young training stable for Vinery, a Lexington, Kentucky-based breeding farm, but that assignment failed to engage him enough so he went looking for another job.

Matz spotted him galloping horses in Florida and was immediately intrigued by Brette's quiet demeanor and light touch on a horse and asked him to stop by his barn in Palm Beach Downs to talk about the future. Matz offered him a job, and soon enough Brette was on the back of Barbaro, wondering where King Kong had come from and where he was going.

"The first day I sat on him, I thought he was a three-year-old," Brette said. "Not just because he was so big but because he was so well-balanced. He was pretty backward and immature, but he always had that big, long stride. I knew he was a nice horse."

Matz relied on the lessons he learned from feeding horses for Bernie Traurig, riding sale horses for Vince Dugan, and putting in countless show-jumping rounds — don't rush them, let them develop in their own time. If you take something out of the tank, put it back in before releasing the valve again. Barbaro wasn't a precocious two-year-old with sights on six-furlong stakes at Saratoga in August. No, training this colt would require a slower approach, one that would take into account Barbaro's growth spurts. More Mother Nature than Michael Matz.

A two-year-old racehorse can go through more ups and downs than the stock market, both mentally and physically. When one comes as big and as talented as Barbaro, it's imperative that a trainer listens to his horse. Barbaro was cut from a dangerous cloth; his big body and his natural speed

---

Peter Brette, a retired jockey, became Barbaro's rider in the mornings

combined for a combustible recipe. The horse could run; that was obvious to Brette every time he opened his hands, but the colt's body was still catching up to his ability. One week a horse can be handling everything; the next he can be struggling with the workload.

Matz recognized that Barbaro was immature. Like his half brother Holy Ground, Barbaro could be antsy coming on and off the track. But as he matured mentally, he grew into his physical frame and each workout became easier. Indeed he seemed to find new gears, Brette observed.

Barbaro worked with another of Matz' two-year-olds, Pegasusbystorm, who went on to win a small stakes at the Meadowlands. Barbaro handled his workmate like a sparring partner.

In the summer of his two-year-old year, Barbaro experienced a growth spurt, and Matz gave him some time off. When he returned to training, Barbaro was even more impressive.

It takes a serious horse for a retired jockey to think about coming back and riding races. Barbaro had Brette, who hadn't ridden a race since 2000, thinking about it. The feeling of a good horse is the only thing a retired jockey misses when it's all said and done. The horse that makes riding easy, one with intelligence to see what is unfolding in front of him, and one with ability that can do something about it. Barbaro was all this.

"Michael talked to me about it, and I thought about it," Brette said. "I would have loved to have ridden him in the afternoon but knew it probably wasn't the right thing to do."

Jose Caraballo heard about Barbaro from a friend who

At Fair Hill, Barbaro's education continues

worked in the Matz barn. The forty-year-old journeyman jockey hustled to Fair Hill to check in with Matz, with whom he had built a healthy working relationship since moving his tack from Suffolk Downs to Delaware Park in 2000.

Caraballo, in helmet and boots just in case, leaned on the wooden rail at Fair Hill and watched Barbaro breeze a routine five-eighths of a mile. Brette crouched behind Barbaro's neck, perfectly tucked into his long stride as Barbaro's long stride clicked off the furlongs as systematically as an odometer.

"He was a great mover, just a beautiful animal," Caraballo said. "I loved the way he worked that morning. As a rider, that's all you do, look for good horses."

Matz gave Caraballo the call for an October 4 maiden race for two-year-olds on the turf at Delaware Park. Barbaro had worked well on the dirt, but Matz decided to unleash Barbaro on the turf after considering his pedigree and his conformation. By renowned turf sire Dynaformer, Barbaro was a natural for the turf and with his size and temperament, Matz wanted Barbaro to debut going a route of ground, which is easier to tackle on the grass than on the dirt. The race also fit perfectly into Barbaro's schedule. Matz met Caraballo in the paddock at Delaware Park, a short ship from Barbaro's Fair Hill base. Matz shook hands with Caraballo while monitoring Barbaro in the tree-filled paddock. Good horses don't need instructions, and Matz didn't say a lot to Caraballo.

"Michael is very quiet; he never told me anything, just that he was a nice colt, that he does everything right, you'll like him," Caraballo said. "He acted like he wasn't that high on him at first, but the way he ran — he got very high on him."

Barbaro gets plenty of time to mature mentally

Sent off as the fourth choice at 7-1, Barbaro broke near the outside in the eleven-horse field and tucked behind Shadwell Farm's Haajes. He contentedly sat in second before rolling to the lead when Caraballo cued the drum roll. Barbaro crushed his overmatched rivals by eight and a half lengths, finishing the mile distance in 1:35 4/5, promising big things with his facile score.

"He did everything right; the moment he started running, you could tell he was different," Caraballo said. "He won so easy; he was such a powerful animal. It was just a gallop for him. It was a great feeling."

Caraballo had carved out a steady living as a jockey since emigrating from Puerto Rico in 1984. He did his time at the roughshod Thistledown in Ohio and Suffolk Downs near Boston before finally landing at Delaware Park. Caraballo had collected more than 2,000 wins, all the hard way. With his consistency he had become a dependable jockey at Delaware Park, often used by top local outfits such as Matz, Michael Dickinson, and Graham Motion. He broke Wood Memorial winner Tapit's maiden and breezed 2005 Kentucky Derby favorite Bellamy Road for Dickinson, but he had never kept the ride on a serious horse.

Six weeks after Barbaro broke his maiden so impressively, Matz signed up Caraballo again, this time for the colt's stakes debut in the Laurel Futurity.

"We didn't know we had a Kentucky Derby horse, I didn't anyway, but we knew we had a nice horse," Caraballo remembered. "I knew he was probably the best horse I had ever been on; he was awesome."

For the first time in its history, the Laurel Futurity was run on the turf, providing a perfect springboard for

In his debut at Delaware Park, Barbaro leaves his challengers far behind

Barbaro. The two-year-old stakes attracted a thirteen-horse field, but there was just one star. Barbaro broke sharply and quickly secured a forward position. He rated along in second before launching a circling and effortless rally that had him eight lengths clear after 1:40 for the mile and a sixteenth. Diabolical ended up second with Exton third. Barbaro galloped out with ease, his ears indicating he was looking for something else to do.

"It was tremendous, the difference between having a Ferrari and a Volkswagen in your hands. He was so superior," Caraballo said. "Johnny Velazquez was in there, Ramon Dominguez, Edgar Prado, they were riding nice horses and I went by those guys like they were riding bicycles."

The race gave Matz a good idea of just what kind of a

racehorse he had on his hands.

"I thought the only way we were going to get beat was by experience. He's pretty nice; at least, he's shown us all the time that he wants to be a nice horse," Matz said after the win. "He's never put a foot wrong ... He's a big, strong colt, and he's done everything we've asked."

But all of this was accomplished on the turf — a surface that doesn't measure up in American racing. Turf is an asterisk to a horse's career. The dirt is where the real money is made — on the track and in the breeding shed. Matz had choreographed two perfect experiences for Barbaro to begin his career saying that the first race happened to come up perfectly in his schedule, and, well, the Laurel Futurity's purse and proximity were too good to be true after Barbaro's maiden turf win. But after two flawless turf performances, Matz wasn't ducking the dirt question; he was actually bringing it up.

"We're going to try him some time, that's for sure," Matz said after the Laurel Futurity.

Barbaro had always worked well on the dirt, and Matz figured that an appearance on the main track was in the cards. Barbaro's dam had run on the dirt, and his half brother was adept on both surfaces.

Edgar Prado happened to be at Laurel on the day of the Laurel Futurity. There to ride the feature, the grade I Frank De Francis Dash, Prado picked up a ride in the Futurity, and it was nothing more than a ringside seat. He watched the developments in front of him as Ramon Dominguez on Diabolical crept up to Barbaro's flank as the horses left the backside.

"I was lying about sixth or seventh," Prado said. "I saw a horse traveling well; Ramon's horse was making a nice bold

move, and he thought he was going to blow by him [Barbaro]. Caraballo just smooched. I said, 'Holy cow.' I hadn't seen a horse with that kind of acceleration since Kitten's Joy. I was impressed."

Kitten's Joy copped the Eclipse Award as best turf horse in the country in 2004, using a turn of foot that left older horses in his wake. Prado, who had ridden the colt to two of his victories, had felt that acceleration then and had been searching for it ever since. Prado drove home from his old stomping grounds at Laurel and called his agent, Bob Frieze, to tell him about Michael Matz' big bay colt who won on the grass.

"I talked to Bob and said this is a nice horse, trained by Michael Matz," Prado said. "At the time, Michael Matz and Bob didn't get along so well, he mentioned that he never returns his phone call. I told him, 'Please, call him again.' "

Matz and Frieze had gotten in a tiff over Kicken Kris in the 2004 Arlington Million when the agent did what agents are paid to do, taking Prado off Matz' horse late to have him ride another horse in the grade I stakes. All turned out fine for Matz when Kicken Kris and jockey Kent Desormeaux were elevated to the win after a steward's inquiry disqualified

---

Barbaro's facile victory in the Laurel Futurity inspires Derby dreams

the first horse. But, still, Matz wasn't calling Frieze.

A few weeks after Prado had first eyed Barbaro, the jockey received the call he had been hoping for. It wasn't from his agent, though; it came directly from Matz. The trainer had left a message for Prado, imploring the jockey, who was in Japan, to call him. Prado immediately phoned Matz and was thrilled to commit to ride Barbaro in the Tropical Park Derby.

"That's how I got the ride; I gave him the call myself," Prado said.

For Caraballo, losing the ride felt inevitable.

"I was hoping to stay on him. I told Michael I'd go anywhere to ride this horse," Caraballo said. "I wasn't upset, I was disappointed, but that's part of the game. As a young guy, I would have gotten upset, but I've learned as I've gotten older. I understand it. I was hoping he would win the Triple Crown, at least it'd be in the books that I rode him."

Matz and Brette had already sketched a blueprint leading to the first Saturday in May — one more race on the turf, the Tropical Park Derby on New Year's Day, then two races on the dirt, maybe the Holy Bull and the Florida Derby. Then the Kentucky Derby.

They knew if he couldn't handle the dirt, there was always turf. And if he could handle the dirt? Look out.

Road to Kentucky

With the Laurel Futurity tucked away, Barbaro joined the annual caravan of talented horses headed south for better weather. In November, Barbaro settled into Matz' barn at Palm Meadows Training Center to prepare for the key Florida preps, which ultimately propel a few colts to the Derby while bestowing a hard reality on the rest. Of the 427 horses that went into the winter season to follow the Kentucky Derby trail, only twenty wouldn't be cast off the exit ramps.

While some trainers rested the more proven members of the upcoming Derby class for their three-year-old campaigns, Matz continued to look down the road for Barbaro's next race. He decided on the grade III Tropical Park Derby at Calder on New Year's Day. The mile and an eighth distance lent itself to Barbaro's innate stamina and provided another mile marker on the road to the Derby. With just two races — two exceptionally easy races — as a two-year-old, Barbaro needed the work and experience. Some of his future rivals already had run five or six times and deserved a brief freshening, such as the highly regarded First Samurai and the talented California-based Brother Derek, but with Barbaro's light work load thus far, there was no reason to

freshen Barbaro for the Derby prep races.

With Edgar Prado aboard for the first time, Barbaro proved to be the same horse who had dominated two Mid-Atlantic starts. Finding a perfect spot just off the lead in the twelve-horse field, Barbaro handled everything like an older horse. He used his natural speed to get a position and his cruise control to keep it. His explosive late speed turned the race into a romp. Barbaro collared Mr. Silver at the head of the stretch and lengthened his already expansive stride to roll home by a commanding three and three-quarters lengths, while finishing the nine furlongs in 1:46 3/5 on firm turf.

"We got a perfect trip, but regardless of that, I could have been anywhere in the race I wanted to be and still would have won," Prado said. "That's how good this horse is. I watched his first two races, and I was impressed. Now, after riding him, I'm even more impressed."

The victory was certainly as impressive as his first two, just another afternoon of play for Barbaro. Still, there were questions. Mostly, the surface. The Tropical Park Derby continued Barbaro's dominance on the turf. Assured by his horse's prowess on that surface, Matz still didn't shy from the issue of dirt, often bringing it up himself.

"He's obviously a very talented horse," Matz said after the Tropical Park Derby. "Whether he carries the class he shows on turf over to the dirt, we just don't know yet, but his mother and half brother [Holy Ground] ran well on the dirt. So, we'll talk it over with the Jacksons to see whether we try him on dirt next."

In keeping with his style, Matz refused to get carried away by the victory. A rational thinker at all times, he constantly evaluates what's in front of him, plotting his next course of action like a United Nations official.

A couple of days after the Tropical Park Derby, Matz told Prado to put another pair of goggles on his helmet — the dirt was next. Matz liked the spacing of the grade III Holy Bull Stakes at Gulfstream Park, five weeks after the Tropical Park Derby, and the distance, a mile and an eighth, would provide Barbaro with his fourth two-turn race. In the gradual build-up to tackling the Derby distance of a mile and a quarter, this was a perfect notch in the sequence.

Though impressed with Barbaro's ability — at least on the turf — Prado was admittedly skeptical about Matz' confidence. Prado said, "He was planning on running the horse in the Kentucky Derby even though he hadn't run on the dirt yet. I thought, 'Wow, the horse is three for three on the turf and he's going to put him on the dirt?'"

Matz, steadfast as ever, knew it was time to put Barbaro to the versatility test. "Don't worry about it," Matz told Prado. "He's working well on the dirt; we're going to run him on the dirt."

Prado couldn't help but think of all the turf horses that exhibited such electric turns of foot on the grass only to lose that acceleration when they tried the dirt. Jockeys aren't paid to look at condition books; they're paid to ride. So Prado rolled through January with high expectations for Barbaro but maintained a wait-and-see attitude until the colt was put to the test.

Prado already had the ride on Hopeful winner First Samurai, whom trainer Frank Brothers was pointing for the March 4 Fountain of Youth. Todd Pletcher had tabbed Prado for the rapid but talented Keyed Entry, who was lining up for the Gotham on March 18 and the Wood Memorial on April 8. John Ward was playing catch-up with the talented but inexperienced Strong Contender, whom Prado had guided to an impressive allowance score in Florida. Ward was eyeing the Toyota Blue Grass on April 15.

"I was surrounded by horses, but I was leaning toward Barbaro. He was very impressive; he was a sound horse; he was training well," Prado said. "Michael didn't put any pressure on me. He just said, 'Do what you do, and let's see if we can make the Derby.' That was real nice; it made my life a lot easier."

Unlike a lot of trainers, Matz wasn't worried. He'd let the horses sort each other out, which they always did, knowing full well that all Barbaro had to do was keep winning for Prado to keep riding him.

Prado gave Matz the call for the Holy Bull on February 4, still wondering whether Barbaro could transpose his long, dominant stride to the dirt.

"Sometimes horses that handle the turf so well, sometimes they run okay on the dirt," Prado said. "He was extremely good on the turf, outstanding. I mean outstanding. I was

Barbaro handles his first race of 2006, the Tropical Park Derby, like a pro

going to work the horse [on the dirt], but, unfortunately, my mother passed away at the same time. I had to go to Peru, so I missed the work."

Like all top jockeys, Prado was in the middle of juggling Derby contenders and wanted to get a feel for the undefeated colt's stride on the foreign surface. His initiation would have to wait until the Holy Bull. And after he had dealt with the toughest thing he'd ever dealt with in his thirty-eight years.

Prado's mother, Zenaida, was his rock. She raised eight sons and three daughters in a one-bedroom, twelve-bunkbed house in Lima, Peru, and had to say goodbye to four of the children who came to America looking for bigger things. Prado left for one reason — to make it big in America.

He didn't let his mother down.

Prado won his first race aboard Tatin in October 1983, and in three years he had become leading rider in Peru. But he always knew he had to leave for the real money in America. The nineteen-year-old booked a one-way ticket to Miami, hugged his mother, and never looked back.

Prado arrived in 1986, signing a contract to ride for trainer Manny Azpurua in Florida. Self-assured but never cocky, Prado could ride and could work.

Like most jockeys, Prado moved from track to track. Miami to Boston to Baltimore, which he would call home for most of the '90s, dominating the competitive colony. Prado was leading rider on the Maryland circuit five times from 1991 to 1997.

In 1999 Prado made the big move, saying goodbye to his playground in Maryland and tackling New York to ride for

---

Barbaro handles his first race on the dirt, the Holy Bull, with aplomb

trainer John Kimmel, who needed a steady rider to take the place of the injured Richard Migliore.

Prado came to town with his tack bag and his work ethic. He started picking up winners just like he had been doing in Maryland. These weren't even-money shots like he consistently steered in Maryland; these were horses meant to be a notch below what Jerry Bailey, John Velazquez, and Pat Day were sitting on during the six-week meet at Saratoga. By the end of the sojourn, Prado had clawed his way to second-leading rider behind Bailey. Maryland was nothing but a memory. Prado showed he belonged in New York and never left.

With 536 wins, Prado led the nation in victories in 1997 and did it again over the next two seasons. He picked up three Saratoga titles and in 2004 became one of about twenty jockeys to ride 5,000 winners. Winless in the Breeders' Cup, Prado broke that drought with two victories in the 2005 Breeders' Cup.

Prado's riding style mirrors his demeanor. Steady. He's never had the buff and polish of Bailey or the muscle and precision of Velazquez — his two biggest rivals since arriving in New York — but if you want the job done, he's your man. No ego, no attitude, and no tantrums. You want fuss or pomp, call someone else; you want results, put him on your speed dial.

He's friendly with everybody, rarely gets visibly upset or excited, takes young riders aside and quietly provides them with lessons. If there's a cause on the backside, just tell him how much money or time is needed and he's there. Prado is the ultimate professional — hard-working in the morning, understated in the afternoon, gracious after the race, and most importantly, brilliant on the racetrack.

Prado enjoys a steady family life with his wife of nineteen years, Lilliana, and three kids — Edgar Jr., nineteen; Patricia, twelve; and Luis, eleven. His mother made frequent extended trips to stay with the family. Prado took her to the Derby to see him ride favorite Harlan's Holiday in 2002 but he could finish no better than seventh. In six tries at the greatest race in America, Prado had yet to get a winner home on the first Saturday in May. In a way, this summed up his career — no big horse.

Prado's mother had a tourist visa for ten years, allowing her to come and go at will. Inexplicably, United States immigration revoked her tourist visa in early 2005. Prado called immigration to figure out why this had occurred and was told that she had been to America too many times.

Prado tried to explain: This is what tourists do; they like a place and they visit there as many times as they want. She didn't work in the country and Prado took care of her. No luck. Prado went to his lawyer, applied for his mother again, and was told it would take a year and a half.

While her papers toiled in a file somewhere in Washington, Prado's mother was diagnosed with breast cancer. Prado escaped to Peru as often as he could while his mother battled her illness. She died on January 19, 2006, at age seventy-six.

"That really bothers me, right here we could have gotten her the best care, the best treatment; that really hurt me," Prado said. "In Peru, she had the care but it's not the same; she didn't really have a fair shot to continue to live."

For Prado, going on without his mother was brutal. He wanted to take some time off from riding but that would be

Victory in the Holy Bull Stakes gives jockey Edgar Prado confidence

against everything his mother told him when he left Peru.

"You have to continue; life is tough, but if you're not tough with life, it will tear you apart," Prado said. "It's hard when you're here; you can win so many races, you can do great, you can be successful, but if you don't share the love or you don't surround yourself with the people you love, what's the point? All for yourself? That doesn't make any sense. You want to share it with your family, your brothers, your mother."

The day his mother died, Prado received a letter approving his mother's visa. It started with, "Welcome to America, you've been approved …"

Later that week Prado flew to Peru for his mother's funeral. He walked to her casket, pulled the letter from his suit, and placed it next to his mother.

"Take this with you, Mom," he said and turned away.

Prado returned to America and to Barbaro.

A twelve-horse field showed up for the February 4 Holy Bull Stakes, but bettors were now enthralled by Barbaro, especially when the track came up sloppy. Oftentimes a sloppy track will pack tight, making it easier for turf horses to negotiate than the loose dirt that can leave them scrambling for traction. Sent off as the 8-5 favorite, Barbaro again broke alertly and settled into a groove just off the leader, Doctor Decherd, who set aggressive fractions of :23, :46 1/5, and 1:10 1/5. Barbaro dispatched Doctor Decherd at the head of the stretch and then held off 25-1 Great Point and My Golden Song to win by three-quarters of a length in 1:49 1/5.

"He broke running, and I had a lot of horse under me the whole way," Prado said. "I turned him loose, and he just

Barbaro's victory in the Florida Derby solidifies his credentials

opened up. He won pretty easy, but he was still a little green, looking for some competition in the stretch. He saw [Great Point] on his outside, but I wasn't ever worried. He proved he could go either way [turf or dirt]."

Matz was happy to see Barbaro clear another hurdle.

"When he saw the lights [at the finish line], he switched leads, but he was never in trouble," Matz said after the race. "God willing, he comes out of the race good, and since we're here in Florida, I suppose we'll look at either the Fountain of Youth or the Florida Derby, or possibly both. We'll let him tell us."

That last sentence said it all. Matz was still going by what his horse wanted instead of memorizing the *Kentucky Derby for Dummies* guidebook, which figuratively says a horse needs to race within a month of the Derby, that he needs more than one race in the thirteen weeks leading up to the Derby, that there was only one way to do it and Matz' way was not it.

With three months to go before the Derby, Matz liked where he stood. Barbaro was four for four and had mastered an adaptable running style that could handle any pace scenario. He had handled the dirt (okay, at least slop). He had the best jockey on the East Coast (and arguably the country) on board.

And Matz had thirteen weeks to tinker with Barbaro's breeze and race schedule. Plus, he had the perfect deputy in Brette, who took the pressure off with his confident handling of Barbaro and his input on everything from race schedule to feeding chart.

Deciding less was better for his big colt, Matz skipped the Fountain of Youth to concentrate on the April 1 Florida Derby. The trainer took the road less traveled with this plan, going against a traditional approach of more races leading up to the Derby. The long-forgotten Needles, the last horse to win the Derby off a five-week layoff back in 1956, kept cropping up in any analysis of the Derby. Still relatively new to racing, Matz couldn't comprehend the hubbub over four weeks or five weeks and set about getting Barbaro to the Florida Derby and — fingers crossed — the Kentucky Derby. Critics be damned.

"Everybody seems to be questioning this or that, but I can't say a single thing bad about the way he's raced or trained," Matz said before the Florida Derby. "He's coming into this race absolutely perfectly, and he's handled everything we've thrown at him."

The Florida Derby would be the test. No turf, no slop, just good old-fashioned American dirt. Classic dirt.

At the break Barbaro bobbled and bumped Charming Image to his inside but quickly solidified that spot of his, just off the pace with dead aim on the leader and first run on the

Barbaro's connections (inset) celebrate his Florida Derby triumph

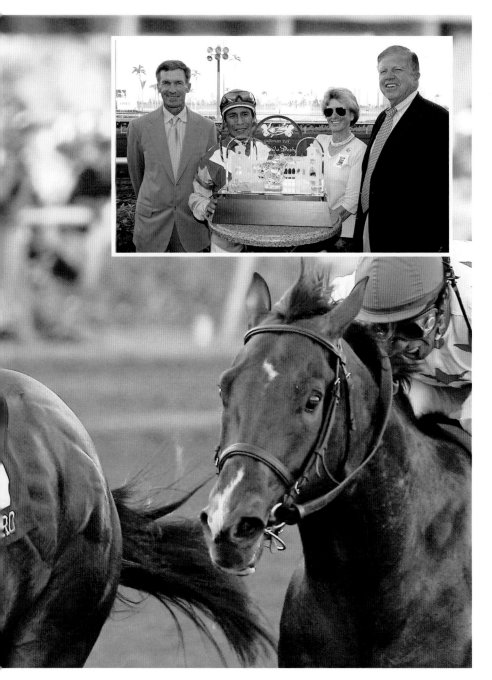

closers. Race after race Barbaro hog-tied his competition in the early going. Prado sat motionless as Barbaro followed fourth-choice Sharp Humor around the first turn and down Gulfstream Park's backstretch. Honest fractions went ticking past — :23 2/5, :47 1/5, 1:11 1/5 — and then it was Barbaro time. Sharp Humor hung tough on the inside, but Barbaro wore him down to win by a half-length in 1:49.

"Everybody thought I was all out, but I never thought about that. He was looking around, there was plenty left in the tank. I felt like he didn't use anything," Prado said. "People said he was all out, he beat a sprinter. They asked me what I thought; all I said was 'definitely.' That was pretty much the beginning of a great story. I had my Derby horse."

Matz had five weeks to wrap Barbaro in cotton and get to the Derby. With Brette at the controls in the morning and Prado all set for the afternoon, Matz was content to keep things the same.

"I asked Michael if he wanted me to get on him in the morning, and he said, 'No, Peter Brette is doing an excellent job,'" Prado said. " 'He gets along with the horse, he loves to get on the horse; he loves to work the horse. If it isn't broke, don't fix it.' "

Brette knew nothing was broken.

As soft-spoken as his boss, Brette remained secure that Barbaro was a Derby horse.

"He's improved from every race. The Florida Derby made a man out of him," Brette said.

Five for five, dirt or turf, Barbaro was on his way to his birthplace, Kentucky, as one of the favorites for the 132nd Kentucky Derby.

Perfect Planning

Matz shipped his undefeated colt to Keeneland on April 12 to work over the Polytrack training track. Rather than send Barbaro to Louisville to get used to Churchill Downs, Matz wanted his horse taking advantage of the forgiving artificial surface of Keeneland's training track and its relative solitude. To some, it appeared an unorthodox way to train for the Kentucky Derby.

Train, he did. Every day Barbaro tipped his hand that something big was about to happen. He sauntered through his daily exercise like a varsity letterman ready for college ball.

Keeneland provides horses with a natural training setting, and Barbaro took advantage of it with each passing morning. There is nothing like a crisp morning in April at Keeneland. Kentucky hardboots have finally kicked the last cobwebs of hibernation from the stark Kentucky winter, and the best stables in the country converge at Lexington's version of Augusta National.

All racetracks collect railbirds at the gap of the track, the ones who lean on the rail, drink coffee, and try to talk horses. But Keeneland attracts the equine cognoscenti — owners, trainers, breeders, jocks' agents, writers, fans who come to see a proper horse going about his morning paces. These aren't tourists.

Sure, some are out there for the atmosphere or sniffing around for a bet or just doing what they do, but all of them, even subconsciously, are there to see the makings of a horse like Barbaro.

The railbirds at Keeneland congregate along a white board fence that provides first-row balcony seating to the morning's activities on the training track. That's where the action happens. Horse deals are made and broken while horses, trainers, and riders are analyzed from afar. Everybody talks horses.

And every morning Barbaro stopped the conversation.

The veterans of a few mornings would nod their heads and elbow the neophytes who hadn't seen him yet, "There's Barbaro."

Then they'd watch, impossible not to stare at the deliberateness of his motion, the size of his stride, the look in his eye — just different than the majority of treadmill horses going through their daily routine over Keeneland's five-furlong training track.

Each morning Barbaro strolled down the slight incline to the training track and walked through the gap. Before turning in toward the track, he would make his own space just past the gap. He'd stand there for minutes, eyeing his world before heading clockwise around the track, known in racetrack parlance as "the wrong way." It was the only wrong way Barbaro was going. Usually after about a mile jog, he'd turn in again, stand for a few moments, and then melt into his perfect long stride for a mile and a quarter gallop. All with the capable guidance of Brette, perfectly at ease, sitting as if he were on his favorite couch.

Each morning, as Barbaro came off the gap, observers stared, gawking at the giant and trying to make some sort of small talk. Just to relay their awe.

"Man, he's got some jog," a writer said to Brette, as the duo caromed off the gap after an effortless two turns around the training track.

"Ha. You should feel his gallop," Brette said, with awe in his voice.

Matz kept Barbaro training over the cushioned Polytrack surface, just the right thing for a turf-to-dirt horse, for most of his two weeks at Keeneland. Barbaro tended to gallop stronger than most other horses; his routine gallops would take him faster than most other horses. With this in mind, Matz breezed him just once while at Keeneland, an easy five furlongs in 1:01 2/5 over the main track on April 23, thirteen days before the Derby. The move was the third fastest of eight breezes, just a maintenance spin, slow but exactly what he needed. The horse couldn't have trained better during April.

Barbaro takes in his new surroundings at Churchill Downs

Keeneland proved to be the perfect segue from training center to racetrack for Barbaro. Up until then Barbaro had lived at four different places: Sanborn Chase, Stephens Training Center, Fair Hill Training Center, and Palm Meadows. Though he had been to the track on race days, he had never heard the continual chatter of an afternoon announcer, never seen horses coming and going to the races all afternoon, never dealt with the relentless buzz of a racetrack. Keeneland exposed Barbaro to a toned-down version of the Derby maelstrom that awaited him at Churchill.

"When we went to Keeneland, he improved so much. He turned into a man," Brette said. "Keeneland was a great transition for him; there were more people there than at the training center. It took him three or four days to get used to Keeneland. Then, it took him about two days to get used to Churchill."

The 2006 Derby attracted a deep and talented field, one of the best collections of horses in its long and storied history. It is America's race, the one race that reaches across the boundaries of an insider's sport. Win the Derby and you've made it.

At least ten horses held legitimate shots at winning the $2 million stakes and another ten were trying to pull off an upset like the unheralded Giacomo had done the previous year.

Barbaro shared the most attention with California's Brother Derek, Oaklawn Park's Lawyer Ron, and Maryland-based Sweetnorthernsaint. Outside of those four came a coterie of horses — some who had shown they, at least, belonged and others who were looking for a miracle. Bluegrass Cat was impressive until his last two when he lost

With the Twin Spires in the background, Barbaro pauses on the track (opposite) and stretches his legs (above)

a shoe in the Tampa Bay Derby and ran flat in the Blue Grass. Three-time Derby winning trainer Bob Baffert came to town with three chances: Blue Grass winner Sinister Minister, Wood Memorial winner Bob and John, and the steady Point Determined. Late runners like Jazil and Steppenwolfer hoped the ten furlongs would wipe out the speed in front of them.

Brother Derek had done nothing wrong while beating up on California's shallow pool of three-year-olds. A winner of four in a row and unbeaten in three starts at three, Brother Derek looked impressive winning his Derby prep, the Santa Anita Derby on April 8. A son of the little-known California sire Benchmark, Brother Derek trounced four rivals while controlling the pace and galloping home when called upon.

A California-bred owned by Cecil Peacock, Brother Derek liked to set or stalk the pace in his races and promised to add heat to the Derby pace that was boiling over with sprinters at heart such as Keyed Entry, Sinister Minister, and Sharp Humor, who had made Barbaro work in the Florida Derby.

Brother Derek's trainer, Dan Hendricks, was confined to a wheelchair after a dirt-bike accident in 2004, and jockey Alex Solis had returned from his own back injury, sixteen days after Hendricks' crash, to regain a prominent spot among the sport's elite. Both were searching for their first Derby victory.

The over-achieving Lawyer Ron streaked through Oaklawn Park's Derby preps in the mold of 2004 Derby winner Smarty Jones. The light chestnut colt had won six in a row, including running the table of three stakes at Oaklawn, his winter base. Unorthodox for sure, Lawyer Ron had a tendency to pull in

---

Gretchen Jackson visits Barbaro at Churchill Downs

his races and at times made jockey John McKee look like George Jetson when Astro took off on the dog walk.

Like most of the major Derby contenders, the connections of Lawyer Ron had stories to tell, too. Old-school trainer Bob Holthus had recovered from open-heart surgery a year earlier while Lawyer Ron's owner, James Hines Jr., had died in a swimming pool accident in February. Stonewall Farm, an up-and-coming Kentucky breeding farm, had purchased a majority interest in the son of Langfuhr, for a reported $6 million, leading up to the Derby and planned to stand him at stud at the finish of his racing career.

Sweetnorthernsaint came out of the maiden claiming ranks to become a legitimate contender on Derby trail 2006 for trainer Michael Trombetta. The Derby rookie learned the game the hard way, investing his and his working-class family's money into the sport. Trombetta had made more trips to Penn National and other egg-and-spoon tracks than he ever cared to remember.

In his debut at two at Colonial Downs, Sweetnorthernsaint got away from his groom and ran loose in the stable area before coming to the paddock. Once in the paddock he was unruly. At the gate he refused to load and eventually finished twelfth of fourteen. After the race, Trombetta took over the training. He told owners Joe Balsamo and Ted Theos that he was castrating the rogue immediately. Trombetta brought him back in a December maiden claimer, which he won by double digits but was disqualified for interference at the start. The gelding won the Illinois Derby in his final Derby prep and had speed-figure gurus reaching for their billfolds.

"What's most enjoyable about this game is that opportunity could very much be around the corner. It could be special,

and you just don't know it's there," Trombetta said before the Derby. "This horse, he went from having all the issues in the world to a stakes winner and hopefully a future stakes winner right on down the line. You just don't know what's around the corner. His first race was a horror story: He got

Getting schooled in the paddock (above) and getting his daily bath

loose; he dropped the rider; he kicked the blacksmith."

Now Sweetnorthernsaint was favorite for the Kentucky Derby.

Matz shipped Barbaro to Churchill Downs a week before the Derby. The trainer wanted one breeze over the Churchill strip, a half-mile tightener to stretch the colt's legs and get a blow into his lungs. It might have been the greatest breeze in the history of the Turf. On his third birthday, one week before the Derby, Barbaro bounded down the Churchill Downs stretch like a kid let out for summer vacation. He made dirt look like turf, skipping over the top of the ground, blazing a half-mile on the fast track in forty-six seconds, the fastest of sixty-nine works that morning. Barbaro galloped out five furlongs in :59 2/5 and finished six furlongs in 1:12 1/5.

Prado was enthralled. Matz was relieved. Brette was agog.

"This will win the Kentucky Derby," Brette said to Matz when he pulled up Barbaro on the Churchill Downs backside. "He felt as though he went down there in three strides."

Funny, to most observers it only looked like two strides. Prado, still riding at Belmont Park, saw the breeze on TVG's program *The Works*.

"I was very impressed," Prado said. "He was just reaching, reaching, reaching. Just cruising, :46 and change in hand, I just said, 'wow.'"

Barbaro cooled out, ate his lunch, his dinner, his breakfast … and remained on simmer for Saturday's Derby. He walked the shed row the next morning and then went back to work, showing off all week. With that breeze over, Barbaro's preparation was down to a routine paddock school, a couple of more gallops, and the finalization of race strategy that Matz would ultimately leave to Prado and Brette.

Barbaro is momentarily uncooperative in the schooling stall

As Matz ticked all the boxes of Barbaro's perfect Derby preparation, more and more people were paying attention.

Matz was relatively new to the Derby scene and perhaps was a little unprepared for the onslaught of reporters that appeared at his barn every morning. The media had taken notice because Matz had a story, one of relatively epic proportions — former Olympian, plane crash hero, undefeated colt — it made for great copy. Matz, gracious and cool as ever, perhaps to a fault, continually had to resurrect the memories of that horrific day in an Iowa cornfield.

"That stuff has been documented," Matz said. "It's one thing if it happened five years ago, but seventeen years, I feel like it's over. I understand the reporters want to make a story and they can do that. I have nothing against that — they're just doing their job — but it's been written about, reported about."

As guests of Churchill Downs, the three siblings Matz had helped would be in Louisville to watch the Derby from a box in section 318, right at the finish line. The regurgitation of the tragic event never rested, but Matz tried to see the positive side.

"They seem to be nice kids, seem to be doing real well," said Matz, who would be reunited with the siblings on Derby Day. "I'm glad they're doing well. Nobody knows how you're going to react, and you just try to do the best you possibly can."

The intense scrutiny Matz and the trainers of other top Derby contenders faced during Derby week didn't let up after all the major breezes were finished. Attention merely turned to the post-position draw. With twenty horses bombarding the first turn, post position is vital. Inside, you get trapped. Outside, you get fanned. Middle, you've still got to get lucky. Matz and Prado spoke on the phone about the post-position draw, which

occurred on Wednesday of Derby week. Prado adamantly instructed Matz not to give away anything in the draw.

"I told him I want to be inside. He said, 'Inside?' I said, 'Yeah, he's got enough speed; he's shown that in the two previous races and he's a good horse,'" Prado said. "The only thing I asked, 'Listen, if for any reason, he doesn't break good and the dirt hits him, I want him to be able to handle it.' He said, 'Don't worry about that; we've been training the horse, the dirt's been kicking in his face, and he's taken everything

---

Barbaro's strides eat up the track

really well. Don't worry.' That was good."

Matz wanted number 4, but when that was gone, he chose stall 8 for Barbaro, inside enough to save ground, outside enough to avoid the bottlenecks that can occur going into the first turn. The other major contenders wouldn't be within a Zip code of the inside gridlock. Sweetnorthernsaint drew the 11, Lawyer Ron accepted the 17 slot, and Brother Derek would be next to the hotdog stand in stall 18.

By Wednesday night Barbaro had a perfect spot in the gate to complete his perfect preparation for the Kentucky Derby.

"Go win our first Derby."

— MICHAEL MATZ TO EDGAR PRADO

King of the Derby

In a thirty-year riding career, Matz had ridden in countless nerve-rattling jump offs, competed in three Olympic games, carried the American flag in the closing ceremonies, and survived a plane crash. Now he was preparing to run a horse in the Kentucky Derby. Not just any horse. A horse he knew had enough talent and class to win the greatest race in the world. The night before, he had gone through the race fifty times, the questions relentlessly rolling through his head. What if Barbaro gets caught in traffic? What if he's dull? ... What if he's sharp? ... Have I done enough? ... Have I done too much?

The same questions repeated themselves rapid-fire through Matz' brain as he ran the gauntlet of Derby Day. Family had to be situated, passes needed to be obtained, a reunion with the Roth children was wedged in the already tight schedule. The media hovered, documenting his every move. Still, Matz couldn't stop going over decisions he had made in the months and days leading up to this moment. His biggest moment in racing.

Finally, the time approached for the trainer to settle down to the business of getting his horse ready to run. Matz made his way through the crowd and onto the tightly packed main track to join Barbaro and Brette, who were waiting back at the barn. Though by himself and preoccupied by his thoughts, Matz was surrounded by a crush of owners, trainers, writers, and eager spectators, all trekking to the stable area to prepare for the Kentucky Derby walk.

About halfway around the Churchill Downs' clubhouse turn, Matz, perfectly pressed in a dark suit, stopped. He knew he had made a mistake. He waffled, visibly stressed for the first time all week, as he gazed back toward the grandstand. Then he started walking that direction — away from the barn and against the crowd.

A friend asked him where he was going. Matz shook his head with a tinge of exasperation.

"My son, Alex, wanted to walk over with me, and I told him no; I just thought there would be too much going on for him," Matz said. "Then as I was walking, I got to thinking, 'I might not ever get here again.' My first Olympics, I didn't even go to the opening ceremonies, I said, 'Oh, I'll be here every year.' It took me sixteen years to get back. After that, I was the first guy on the bus."

Nine-year-old Alex Matz neatly attired in a khaki suit, spotted his father and ducked under the rail and grabbed his dad's hand. The smile on Alex's face was worth a thousand Derbies. Father and son, hero and son, walked back to the barn where Barbaro awaited.

As Matz finally got to his horse, the Jacksons were dividing to separate barns. Roy Jackson headed right to Tony Reinstedler's barn where Showing Up was stabled, and Gretchen Jackson took a left to barn 42 where Barbaro had been stabled for the week. The Jacksons had come to

Matz and son Alex make "The Walk"

Churchill for the 132nd Kentucky Derby with two guns blazing. Along with Barbaro, came undefeated Showing Up, who had shown up late with a lively effort, in Keeneland's Lexington Stakes, just two weeks before the Derby. Trainer Barclay Tagg, conservative to the point of stubbornness, was impressed enough with Showing Up's development to give the Jacksons a second horse to root for in the Derby. Gretchen had first pick, so she chose to walk with Barbaro while Roy accompanied Showing Up.

"We're just trying to enjoy it. This is a lifelong dream; then, to have two horses …" Roy Jackson said, moments before walking over with Showing Up. "It goes by so fast. Someone said it's like a wedding. We're just trying to soak it in and enjoy it. I had never seen a race here. When I was in baseball, I snuck in here one day to see it [the track], when it was dark, that's all."

It had already been a big day for the Jacksons, who earlier that morning, in their hotel lobby, had watched homebred George Washington win the Two Thousand Guineas, first leg of the English Triple Crown. The Jacksons had sold George Washington to world giant Coolmore, for $2 million.

But George Washington wasn't in their silks and, certainly to an American, the Two Thousand Guineas is not the Kentucky Derby. The big one they wanted was nearly here.

The announcement, "Bring your horses over for the tenth race. Bring your horses over for the Kentucky Derby," calling the twenty Derby horses to the paddock sent a shiver through Matz and all the other Derby participants. Idle anticipation finally breached to tense activity; at least there was something to do instead of checking equipment and worrying about decisions long since made.

The Barbaro team marched from their barn, Peter Brette, clasping his arms behind his back, leading the way, with Barbaro, in a pair of bell boots to protect his front feet and a set of hind run-down bandages, following about ten yards behind. Matz took his son by the hand and Gretchen Jackson fell into formation. Finally, action.

Barbaro strolled out of the barn like it was his world; free and easy, just like every morning — and every afternoon — in his dynamic career. The prodigy was finally at the place where everyone around him knew he'd be: Churchill Downs for the Kentucky Derby. All those plans, all those decisions, now it was down to minutes to see if they could come to fruition.

The individual Derby horses departed their barns and converged in the mile chute at Churchill Downs where they waited for the next call to the paddock. Matz, his son, and Gretchen Jackson, still surrounded by press, waited, nothing more to say at this point, just stunted small talk in an attempt to quell the nerves.

Every year, this is the first moment when you see all the Derby horses together for the first time. They've prepped in various races around the country, they've brought hopes and dreams of people from around the world, and now here they are, all in one place, circling, waiting. Out of the 37,000 foals in the 2003 crop, here are the best twenty on the first Saturday in May.

"Who wants to be first? Step up to the plate. Okay, come on, amigo," the guard at the edge of the chute begged for the first horse to start the walk. Alex clutched his dad's hand (or was it the other way around?) as the twenty-horse brigade began to make the three-furlong walk toward the paddock.

Peter Brette walked with Barbaro, eyeing everything around him as if he were an undercover bodyguard.

Barbaro did the Derby walk like he did every other walk, in his own world, nothing bothering him, just strolling to do a job, ready for what lay ahead. This is how he handled everything in his career. Turf, slop, dirt? No problem. Kentucky Derby; 150,000 fans; mile and a quarter? Let me at it.

The Derby horses make the walk alongside the crowd, which has ratcheted up its energy in anticipation. Derby fans, many well imbibed by now, form an amphitheater of noise, waving their arms, pumping their fists, and screaming for their choices, thinking the encouragement will help them run faster. The skittish Thoroughbreds somehow handle the chaos and energy.

Late-running Steppenwolfer, with his tongue tied down and nose turned up; Showing Up, like he had run thirty races not just three; Lawyer Ron, tensing up as he entered the tunnel to the paddock; and Barbaro, the composed and confident Barbaro.

Matz followed about ten yards behind Barbaro. Nervous. The twenty horses finished the long, drawn-out procession and entered the paddock. Horses still on simmer, with the paddock and its five-deep crowd, well past boil, ready to see the horses. By this time the paddock was choked with people — owners, trainers, a few celebrities, hangers-on — anticipating the race they had been waiting for all day. And for a few, all their lives.

Matz faced Barbaro toward the back wall of saddling stall

Barbaro is a model of composure in the post parade

number eight. He cinched the girth, and Barbaro replayed his Florida Derby antics, thrusting into the air and unleashing a restrained buck, but ever mindful of the back wall. No problem, just showing who's boss. Barbaro spun around and barged out of the stall before taking a short turn and getting back to his old self.

When he tightened the overgirth around Barbaro's stout barrel and the horse took a turn of the paddock, Matz finally let go of the nerves or at least stowed them somewhere. As an Olympic athlete, Matz had learned how to channel his nerves into something positive, something that would make him ride better. Back then he would walk the course, count the strides, warm his horse up, and enter the ring. The outcome was his responsibility, dependent on his actions, his thoughts. As a Derby trainer, though, the outcome was out of his hands. The outcome was up to Prado — and Barbaro. Matz was still the head coach but he didn't even have a clipboard, a playbook, or a headset, he had nothing but a set of binoculars and the hands of his two small children, Alex and Lucy. For Matz the difference between the Olympics and the Derby was extreme — the simple realization that the Derby was out of his hands while an Olympic show-jumping round was in his hands all the way to the moment Grande or Heisman or Rhum touched down after the last fence. When Matz realized this, his nerves were gone. The great pitcher, Cy Young, once said about pitching, "The ball has left my hand."

And now it was in Prado's capable hands. The jockey was at ease; he had never been so confident for such a big race in his life. This horse made him feel invincible. For a jockey, there is no better feeling in the world than knowing you are on a perfectly prepared rocket ship of a horse. Knowing that

Barbaro and Showing Up (6) race as a team in the early going

he's sound, he's sane, and he has all the tools. It's like knowing you're going to be dealt a handful of aces before you sit down at the table; sure, there's work to be done, but it's a hell of a lot easier when you're holding the right cards. For jockeys riding in the Derby, it's all about putting your nerves somewhere so they can help you, instead of allowing them to alter your natural decision-making.

Barbaro emerged from his paddock stall, and Brette gave Prado a leg up. With Prado in the saddle, Barbaro settled down after that one instance of nervousness in the paddock (Phil Serpe said he got it from his mother, La Ville Rouge, who used to do the same thing) and joined in the post parade without a fuss. Led by the scrappy Jazil, the field headed out of the Churchill Downs paddock, which was a mosh pit of hats, suits, and dangling credentials. The anticipation was palpable, the day having slowly built to the crescendo of the Derby.

As the horses stepped onto the main track the first notes of "My Old Kentucky Home" played and 157,536 people rose to their feet to sing this sentimental state anthem. The applause at the end of the song unnerved Sweetnorthernsaint and Point Determined, who momentarily skidded out of the post parade but then re-joined the walk.

Barbaro continued to handle everything that came his way in front of the madding, dizzying crowd. He was still at ease with his place as his nineteen rivals warmed up around him.

Barbaro loaded into the gate and stood four square in the dirt while the rest of the field filed into line. As Flashy Bull

Sinister Minister (outside) and Keyed Entry lead the pack

made it an even twenty in the gate, Barbaro lifted his right front hoof off the ground. The gate sprang open; he stumbled for a moment and then was off and running, easing into his powerful stride. Showing Up and Barbaro converged for a stride, forcing Wood Memorial winner Bob and John out of the spot and giving the Jacksons one place to watch. Their undefeated pair raced side by side as the field went under the wire the first time.

Keyed Entry yanked jockey Pat Valenzuela to the lead, and Blue Grass winner Sinister Minister rattled fractions too. Sharp Humor broke sharply but stayed wide to avoid a three-way duel on the front end. Prado eased Barbaro into fourth behind the runaway speed of Keyed Entry and Sinister Minister. Showing Up found a cozy spot inside Barbaro as the field went around the first turn. Brother Derek, for one, was already in big trouble, throwing a front shoe and never finding a seam to save ground around the first turn. The rest of the field volleyed in and out of their own snags and crevices, just like in every other Derby, while the horse with the biggest engine, Barbaro, made his own trip.

Prado focused on getting Barbaro comfortable as he had done in the past. With a twenty-horse field it was paramount to get Barbaro in the same position he had enjoyed in his previous races, just off the lead, relaxed and in a cocoon. Prado didn't want to rush Barbaro, but he also didn't want to fade into the middle of the pack where he would be at the mercy of racing luck. When the speedy Sharp Humor stayed outside, it left a big gap, allowing Barbaro to sit in the exact spot Prado wanted. Horse was happy and so was jockey.

Barbaro eases away on the far turn

Prado crouches low and aims for the wire

Barbaro virtually inhales the length of the stretch

Barbaro vanquishes his rivals, crossing the wire in isolated splendor

Just as Matz had said in the days leading to the Derby, Barbaro got himself in the race with ease and staked out a spot — once again the eye of the storm. Somehow, in race after race, Barbaro solidified a position moments after the

Prado extolls the crowd to cheer the Derby winner (opposite) and gives Barbaro a refreshing splash

break, forcing the rest of the field to hover around him. For a big, deliberate-striding, stamina-laden turf horse, he had gears to spare.

"He stumbled a little bit, so I didn't rush him, just let him do his own thing. He started to position himself, easy," Prado said. "I took up my position where I wanted to be; I saved a lot of ground going into the first turn. On the backside, I eased him out to try to avoid as much dirt as possible. You don't want to take that dirt if you don't have to; I was going to go two or three wide anyway. Everything worked out beautiful. He was push button, acceleration then relaxed, acceleration then relaxed."

When Kent Desormeaux sent Sweetnorthernsaint through horses on the backside, Barbaro and Prado never flinched, the jockey pulling his first pair of goggles down and barely reacting to the favorite's dramatic move. Barbaro lobbed along, just off the pace setters and in front of the closers, waiting for the final turn.

"At the half-mile pole, I knew he was going to be really tough; I thought he was going to win for sure," Prado said. "If somebody beats this horse today, he's a super horse, out of this planet. I looked around. I looked inside. I saw Kent rushing with that horse. If he went by me and opened up five, I knew I had him. All I had to do was smooch, and he grabbed the bit and wanted to go, I said, 'Oh, OK, just hold on; we've got three-eighths to go, don't worry about it.' In the Derby? That was exciting."

Just as he had done in his previous five races, Barbaro launched into the race on the turn. Prado snuck a look to his left as Barbaro inhaled Sinister Minister, his jockey Victor Espinoza gawking at Prado, flabbergasted by the quickness

of Barbaro's move. Just like his breeze earlier in the week, Barbaro launched into gear and in a way Brette was right. It looked as though he went down the stretch in three strides. The high knee action that was once criticized, ever present, would never be questioned again. Barbaro was gone.

At the eighth pole Prado turned his whip over and snuck a quick look under his right shoulder. He liked what he saw. With whip at the ready, Prado waved it in rhythm with Barbaro's beat, flicking it for peace of mind more than anything else. It wasn't needed. Barbaro won by six and a half lengths, blitzing the last quarter of a mile faster than any other Derby winner since Secretariat.

Matz, stunned, hugged his daughter Michelle, his son Michael, his wife, his son Alex, his daughter Lucy. Prado pumped his fist once, not in ecstasy but more in confirmation, at the wire and then gave Barbaro a congratulatory slap on the neck, the horse's ears flipping up and back, acknowledging the gesture. Prado couldn't believe he never had to hit the horse, still couldn't believe the gap he saw as he looked under his right arm and saw nothing but fading colors. As Barbaro lowered his landing gear and eased to a walk, Prado looked up at the sky and saluted his mother. The last six months had been tough for a son. On the way back he pumped both fists and pointed at Barbaro, imploring the crowd to cheer on the champ. The big, undefeated colt still had his ears up, looking like he had just gone for a twenty-minute hack up the Goat Hill at Fair Hill.

On the turf course Prado jumped off Barbaro and looked at the almost dumbfounded Matz who stood in amazement

All eyes are on Barbaro as Gretchen Jackson (opposite) leads him in

Matz hoists the Derby trophy and Prado plants a kiss; the Jacksons at the post-race press conference cannot contain their joy

at the sight of his first Derby winner.

"Give me a hug," Prado said to Matz.

Trainer and jockey hugged in celebration of their first Derby victory, exactly what Matz had in mind when he said to Prado in the paddock, "Go win our first Derby." It was Prado's seventh try, Matz' first.

In what was billed as a wide-open affair, Barbaro

dominated the Derby. Bluegrass Cat erased his Blue Grass debacle with a decent effort to collect second. Steppenwolfer galloped steadily to the line to pick up third. Brother Derek circled what he could and finished in a dead heat with stretch-running Jazil for fourth. Sweetnorthernsaint emptied out from his mid-race surge to finish seventh. Lawyer Ron was never in the hunt, winding up twelfth and coming out of the race with a bum ankle.

Prado, the Jacksons, the Matzes (and a gaggle of children and grandchildren) joined Tom Meeker, retiring president of Churchill Downs; David Novak, CEO of Derby sponsor Yum! Brands; and Kentucky Governor Ernie Fletcher in

the winner's circle. No fly-by-night owners who whoop and scream, the whole group graciously accepted the trophy for Barbaro, looking as if they knew they belonged there. NBC's Bob Costas had to worm his way through children to interview Matz, who remained humbled by his role in this incredible horse story. Matz continued to thank his staff at home at Fair Hill and Delaware Park while Prado's thoughts had already moved to the Triple Crown. So had the thoughts of millions of Americans, who longed to see this superhorse assume his place in history. It was apparent that Barbaro was a horse who loved to run, who loved competition, who functioned like a pro at every level on the racetrack. With his unbeaten record, sheer animal charisma, and compelling trainer with a story, Barbaro had become a superstar.

After the race Brette jubilantly walked back to the barn with Barbaro, who was barely blowing from his effort.

A scattered but determined chant began along the outside rail.

"Still undefeated."

"Still undefeated," Brette said in return.

Barbaro's Derby — a tour de force

Barbaro walked away from the winner's circle with a purpose. The same purpose he showed in his first fledgling steps at Sanborn Chase, through lessons at Stephens Training Center, in his five victorious prep races, in those glorious Keeneland gallops, in that sizzling Churchill breeze and finally through the supposed-to-be formidable mile and a quarter of the Derby.

Brette looked at Barbaro in awe. Asked if he was surprised, Brette scoffed.

"No," Brette said. "Not at all, actually.

"He's the best I've sat on and I've been lucky enough to sit on some nice horses," he added. "He's a horse Sheikh Mohammed dreams about; he's his type of horse. I hoped he was as good as I thought he was. I still think he's as good on turf. The world is his oyster; he's that good. And he's still going to strengthen up. You get some horses that are just freaks. He's not just a freak; he's made in all the right ways. He's become a professional now."

As Barbaro walked into the test barn, for post race drug testing, Brette paused at the corner of the barn and tried to sum up the horse. "He's so, so talented. So talented," Brette said.

"And the best is yet to come."

A Fair Haven

With a mile dirt track, a seven-furlong wood-chip track, turn-out paddocks, miles and miles of grass hills, and more deer to dodge than cars, Fair Hill is as close to nature as a horse trainer can get without owning his own spread. The tranquil training center sits on the edge of the 5,600-acre Fair Hill preserve in the northeast corner of Maryland.

The town of Fair Hill, which is more of a crossroad between Newark, Delaware, and Elkton, Maryland, is home to horse lovers. The local lunch spot, Prizzio's Market and Deli, gets the majority of its business from the Mid-Atlantic office of Fasig-Tipton Sales Company, the Thoroughbred Racing Associations, the National Steeplechase Association, and the trainers and staff at the training center. Twice-a-year visitors converge on the town — for an annual steeplechase meet and an international three-day event. When the equine activity dwindles in the winter, Prizzio's business takes a hit.

Fair Hill Training Center, started by Dr. John Fisher in the early 1980s, had weathered plenty of red days, bleeding money with its high overhead. Too small yet too big, the place struggled to find its niche in an industry where free stalls at the racetrack are the norm. Trainers came and went,

barn owners went bankrupt, management folded, and new management tried again. Finally, partly due to Delaware Park's purses being boosted by slot revenue, things started to pick up. With the addition of top-tier outfits like Matz and Graham Motion and about a dozen other dedicated trainers, the upswing continued.

But nobody expected Fair Hill to be welcoming home a Kentucky Derby winner. With his six and a half-length romp, Barbaro let Fair Hill out of the bag. As soon as the Derby was over, people started calling and coming to Fair Hill in droves, looking for the Derby winner, who arrived back at his base at 5:30 Monday morning after an overnight van ride from Churchill Downs.

Fair Hill manager Sally Goswell was one of the few around the training center who didn't watch the Derby from resident veterinarian Kathy Anderson's vet clinic, which adjoins Matz' barn. Goswell celebrated Barbaro's win as she brought her son, John, back from college in North Carolina. When Goswell arrived at work on Monday, she realized things would be different around the country hideaway of Fair Hill. The answering machine was full and so was her e-mail in-box.

"Every time you hang the phone up, it rings again. Someone wants a tour; someone wants this," Goswell said the Tuesday morning after the Derby. "We didn't have a plan; we didn't think we needed a plan. Mid-morning [Monday], I decided we needed a plan."

Goswell called Matz and made the plan. Each morning, barring weather changes, Barbaro would train at about 9:30 and Matz would talk to the press outside his barn from 10:30

Barbaro gets some down time at Fair Hill

to 11:00 (little did he know, most of these sessions would last hours).

"Normally there isn't much of a crowd here in the morning. For Fair Hill, this is packed," Goswell said, surveying a crowd of about twenty tourists searching for Barbaro on Tuesday morning. "We're not trying to promote Fair Hill and we're not trying to keep people out, but people have asked if we're going to have a day like Smarty Jones. They had eight thousand people; I don't think so."

Beyond Barbaro, Matz still had a stable full of horses to train, many of which he needed to catch up with in person, after weeks of traveling with Barbaro.

Media surrounded Fair Hill in all directions, even overhead as television crews in helicopters shot footage of the scene from the sky. All morning, reporters and the curious stopped by Matz' barn to see Barbaro. One tourist marched down the middle of the barn aisle during training hours and plopped down his camera bag.

"Can I help you?" Matz asked.

"No, I'm just here to see Bar Barrow," the man said. "Do you know where he is?"

Matz just shook his head and asked the guy to step outside; the horse would be out in a few minutes. Despite the media blitz around Matz, the trainer went about his business like always — arriving early and leaving late.

Inside his tackroom there was some refuge; it was just Matz and his help. First thing Wednesday morning, four days after the Derby, Matz sat down at his desk in the tack room, placed a battered dry-erase board in his lap, and started marking the set list. His help, including daughter Michelle, hovered, making edits and comments about the morning schedule.

Matz wrote down Barbaro in the fourth set, finished the set list, walked out, and climbed on his pony Messaging to accompany the first group of horses to the track.

Down at the end of the barn, in his old stall, Barbaro bided his time until it was his turn to train. In the stall he was just a horse. Placid and aloof, a splotch of white, like a melting kite, between his eyes, pink snip at the end of his nose. White front feet. Perfect hip, shoulder to match. Big, bay colt who somehow seemed to be able to swell on command. In the Derby paddock he towered above the other nineteen horses. A man among boys, exuding maturity, older than his years. Now, standing in the stall at Fair Hill in the morning, he was big, but not bigger than life.

Hours after Matz wrote up the board, Barbaro ambled to the dirt track for a quiet leg-stretching exercise. He stopped and waited a few paces from the gap of the dirt track, just like he had done every other morning since arriving here as a farm-hyped raw colt, half brother to the big Saint Ballado colt Holy Ground. Matz, Brette, and Barbaro gazed across the infield while horses fidgeted around them. After a patient moment Matz and the foursome broke into an easy jog. Barbaro headed off like he had picked up a lunch pail to go to the factory, just easy motion, steady and unfazed. He exhibited the same composure and consistency that had carried his game from his early education as a two-year-old, through winter training at Palm Meadows, to the week of the Derby, and now back to Matz' home base with ten days to the Preakness.

Training definitively, like he had all spring, Barbaro jogged

Turning out the Derby winner causes a stir

twice around the dirt as Brette marveled at all the horse he had beneath him.

"If he feels this good after four days," Brette told Matz. "Then, holy ****, what he's going to feel like in ten days?"

After a quiet jog and a few spins around the shed row, Matz turned out Barbaro in a grass round pen. Matz slid the brass shank from Barbaro's halter, slipped out of the corral, and waited for the colt to explode. Barbaro whipped around, exuded a barely audible squeal, bent his knees, and folded onto the ground. He rolled back and forth, hopped up, and then put his head down and grazed like he was interviewing for a lawn mower ad.

After passing the small-paddock test (Matz liked trying Barbaro in a more confined area before turning him out in a bigger paddock), Matz turned Barbaro out in a bigger, board-fence paddock, closer to the barn. A Derby winner turned out — wow! Photographers slammed on their motor drives, click, click, click, click. Writers stood in wonder; they had never seen a Derby winner loose — ever.

Just as he said he would, Matz met with the impatient press at the end of training hours. The press ranged from grizzled veterans to teenage interns from the local paper down the street. Instead of questioning Matz about a horrific plane crash or about the daftness of a five-week layoff, the theme had changed to Fair Hill.

The questions about Fair Hill zinged from the ridiculous to the baffling. Reporters couldn't grasp the concept of riding out back in the woods and around the fields, up the "Smelly Hill," over to "Goat Hill," and around to "Chuck's Field" as

Barbaro stretches his legs before the Preakness

the locals call the circuits.

"Has Barbaro gone for these, uh, 'trail rides'?"

"Does he like them?"

"Do you time these workouts?"

"Will he go for one this week?"

Matz took his time, answering the same questions day after day. He finally snapped when asked how long Barbaro had slept the night before but quickly regained his composure and continued to try to put Fair Hill and Barbaro into perspective.

"He got back here, in his old stall; he shipped back well, and today was the first day back to the track and he seemed to enjoy it," Matz said. "You can't turn a horse out that's not used to doing it. He's used to doing it. It doesn't suit everybody, but it suits him. If the horses are happy, they're going to do for us what we ask them to do. The big thing is to try to keep a sound, happy horse."

Patient and articulate as ever, Matz juggled Barbaro, the press, his other fifty horses, family, owners, guests, and phone calls. Constant phone calls. His wife stood in line to ask him a question. The storm was just getting started.

Matz conceded that while he was lucky to have a Derby winner so early in his career, he was struggling to balance the constant attention with the need to maintain a daily routine and care for his horses. "I'm on the phone a lot more, and I was on the phone a lot before," he said. "You just have to keep in touch with the owners, the horses, the veterinarians, the racetracks, the entries, the different things. I'm just trying to take it one step at a time."

Matz takes care not to do too much with Barbaro

Horse owner Rick Porter had called Matz about taking grade I stakes winner Round Pond, who had been off since March and would be pointed to the November Breeders' Cup. Prominent owner Irvin Cowan had called about some two-year-olds he wanted to send Matz: one by Danehill out of Breeders' Cup Distaff winner Hollywood Wildcat, another by pre-eminent sire Elusive Quality, a third by the great Gone West.

"Mr. Cowan called and said, 'I know you take good care of the horses and I appreciate that. My feeling is that it's not so much what you do with them, it's what you don't do with them.' You know, he's right," Matz said. "When I was helping people with the show horses, it wasn't so much what you do with them, it's how not to hinder the horse. Basically, that's the hardest thing to do. I think it was [Charlie] Whittingham who was asked what rider would fit the horse best and he said, 'It's about the rider who will hinder the horse the least.' When you come to think about it, he's right."

Matz retold this story as he and Brette walked back from the track with Barbaro. It was almost as if he were trying to remind himself that he needed to stay out of Barbaro's way, that nothing clever was needed other than to let the horse be a horse. What's meant to happen would happen.

No amount of training savvy would have won Matz the Derby without the right horse. He had the right horse. Now it was a matter of maintaining the level of fitness and confidence that Barbaro had achieved. "I don't think he needs any big works; he'll gallop for sure," Matz said. "Now, we just follow the horse and try to get him to the Preakness as well as possible."

That seemed easy. All the talk, blathered by the media, about five weeks before the Derby, the first horse since Needles, one race in blah, blah, blah weeks … if you stood around and watched Barbaro, the lunacy of statistics, history, and trends was so apparent. This horse was thriving, whether it was five weeks or five days, Barbaro was peaking at the right time, just as Matz and Brette had planned.

"God knows between the eight-week layoff and the five-week layoff, if he didn't run well I would have been the most unorthodox trainer in North America," Matz said. "So far, it's worked out. We'll see what happens."

Quietly confident, the trainer smiled that classic smile that the world was starting to understand means all is well.

The pressure of the Preakness looming hadn't dampened the smile despite the formidable task ahead — win and carry the world for another three weeks like Smarty Jones in 2004; lose and explain the fluke that occurred on the first Saturday in May in 2005 like Giacomo. Not that the horse noticed the enormity.

"You know how many times you plan on doing something and it doesn't work," Matz said to a reporter. "He never wavered at all in his training. He's done everything right so far. Just like today, he might be feeling good, but he jogs around, goes out in the paddock, stands there."

Watching Barbaro stand around like a pony, breathing the fresh air of Fair Hill and listening to Matz talk about horsemanship made the Triple Crown seem so tangible. So attainable. The last time the Triple Crown seemed within reach was when Smarty Jones stood on the precipice after his Derby and Preakness victories in 2004. Preparing for the Belmont, he had galloped stronger and stronger each day, but his innate lack of stamina was hovering like a black cloud. The colt was tense in the cramped quarters of Philadelphia Park and feeling the miles of training. John Servis kept

the flame alive as long as he could, but eventually the wick burned down to nothing. Smarty Jones lost the Belmont in agony and never ran again.

But this time it felt different. If horsemanship counts — fresh air, grass paddocks, breeding — a twelfth Triple Crown winner was more than an elusive dream. Matz relied on old-fashioned horsemanship, trying to keep Barbaro happy with relaxed training methods.

So far, it was working. The ever-sensible Barbaro grazed peacefully in his paddock, occasionally looking at the sets of horses going to and from the training track with an expression that suggested 'Why don't you take me?' Matz marveled that four days previously Barbaro had blazed to glory before 150,000 people and now ate grass like any other horse. "To me, it's common sense," Matz said. "If you ask me to build a rocket ship, I wouldn't have the first clue. But this is an animal, and you try to make sense of it, that's all."

Matz, more horseman than horse trainer, had been making sense with Barbaro's training since the colt arrived at Fair Hill in April of his two-year-old year. Back when Brette got on him for the first time and thought he was a three-year-old. Through his Derby preparation, the one that had the critics atwitter, spooked over a five-week layoff. Matz also went against history and brought Barbaro to the Derby off three turf races to start his career. Why? Because he thought it was the right thing to do by his horse, and his closest allies thought it was the right thing to do.

Matz went easy with Barbaro between the Derby and Preakness, thinking maybe he'd give him one short breeze if

Barbaro remains full of vigor

he was getting too fresh but otherwise just relying on a few jogs and a few gallops to get him to Pimlico. Barbaro's routine during the two weeks from the Derby to the Preakness made perfect sense to anyone who has tried to think like a horse. It was a glorious two weeks for Team Matz.

The Derby was stowed away. Barbaro was sound, at his home base after six months on the road, and getting better by the day.

Matz couldn't help but talk about the potential of Barbaro. That's how good his Derby had looked — like he hadn't reached his potential. A six and a half-length tour de force, untouched by the whip, by a horse making his sixth career start. Like Brette said, the world was his oyster.

"Even after the Derby, you don't know how good he is; maybe we haven't seen the best of this horse yet," Matz said. "He's an April 29 foal; he might just be getting better. There's a lot of things to look forward to in this horse. He's the type of horse that people want to see do well. I'm not saying he's Secretariat but maybe he is; it's fun to think about that. He can get compared to horses like Secretariat, Seattle Slew, the great horses of our era. I'm looking forward to the Preakness — if we get past the Preakness, the Belmont. I think this horse can win the Triple Crown. I think the public is looking for somebody to do that, and I hope he's the one."

Two days before the Preakness, Brette let Barbaro roll through the stretch of the dirt track at Fair Hill. The horse moved effortlessly, reaching for ground just like he had in all his other breezes and races.

The Triple Crown was getting warmer.

Preparations for the Preakness are complete

Day of Despair

The day before the Preakness, Horse of the Hour Barbaro and longshot Diabolical departed the relative solitude of Fair Hill Training Center for the sixty-mile trip to Pimlico. Matz had contemplated shipping Barbaro to Pimlico on Saturday morning but didn't dare tempt fate and decided Friday afternoon was cutting it close enough.

The Brook Ledge van arrived at Pimlico at about 2:40. A crowd of about two hundred racing fans and media stood waiting, trying to catch a glimpse of Barbaro as Eduardo Hernandez led the Preakness favorite off the van.

The big horse was on the grounds, providing the first tangible evidence that it was, finally, time for the 131st Preakness. In four white bandages, bell boots to protect his front shoes, bay coat glistening as if he had just stepped out of an Armor All commercial, Barbaro made a couple of routine circles around the Pimlico stakes barn before settling into stall 40, traditionally reserved for the Derby winner. Nearing the twenty-four-hour mark, Barbaro appeared honed and ready for his seventh straight victory.

Saturday morning Matz knew Barbaro needed some exercise to settle down the energetic youngster. Under Brette,

Barbaro galloped easily around Pimlico's oval. His two white feet, four navy polo bandages, white shadow roll, and light-blue Preakness saddle towel cut a perfect vision through the morning air. It was trademark Barbaro: head down, legs locomotion-efficient, furlongs ticking past quicker than mile markers on a westbound turn-around. Everything appeared to be in place.

Matz still marveled at his charge, thinking that it would take a hell of a horse to beat him.

Prado wasn't there to see the gallop, but he was full of confidence himself. He discounted the idea that after such a good race in the Derby and a short layoff — the shortest of Barbaro's career — that the horse would fail in the Preakness.

"After the Derby there were people talking about the 'bounce,' " Prado said. "It never crossed my mind. He did everything on his own power. He wasn't all out; he had never been all out. There was plenty left, so much left. That theory could not apply to Barbaro."

Without a doubt, Prado, Matz, and the Barbaro team knew that Pimlico provided the toughest element of the

Triple Crown. It was a matter of just trying to get past this leg, to avoid getting trapped or roughed up over Pimlico's speed-favoring, tight-turn oval. Once this one was over — like a dentist's appointment — it would be full speed ahead to Belmont Park, a track made for Barbaro's sweeping, bounding stride and a distance suited to his pedigree. Barbaro at Belmont, going a mile and a half; round peg in a round hole. Nothing seemed to fit better than that.

A record crowd of 118,412 turned out on a perfect spring day at Pimlico. Barbaro's popularity aside, they weren't all there to see him. The Preakness provides a day out, a rite of spring around Baltimore; the infield opens up, and it looks more like spring break than a horse race.

But, for those that came to see a horse, there was only one that mattered. The press, horsemen, and fans amassed at the stakes barn to see off the burgeoning champion. Not that they could see much behind Pimlico's dense green awning that hid stall 40, but they waited intently for a glimpse of Barbaro.

With Showing Up shaking off his fifth-place Derby effort (and awaiting a turf career) at Belmont Park, the Jacksons could make this walk to the paddock together. Roy Jackson looked at the writer who had walked over with him for the Derby and motioned toward the wood-chip horse path that runs along Rogers Avenue.

"Come on; let's do this again," Jackson said. "Let's hope we have the same luck."

Barbaro strolled down the path, along the edge of the Pimlico stable area and around the hordes of fans that converge every year by the head of the stretch. They know the Derby winner and root their approval.

"I'd sure like to do this every year," Matz said to Roy Jackson as the big horse stepped onto the turf course to be saddled for the Preakness.

Prado, dressing in a corner of the Pimlico jocks' room, slid on his navy Tipperary safety vest and tucked Lael's white, blue, and green silks into his breeches. He adjusted his helmet cover and goggles and mentally went through the race:

He always breaks well; he puts me in the race; he's got plenty of speed ... Watch getting pinned down on the inside, should be a little bit of speed to sit behind. Like Now's going; they'll probably send Brother Derek; Sweetnorthernsaint's quick. On the best horse in the race, don't get him in trouble ... and remember Funny Cide and Smarty Jones who drew off and ran too hard in this leg; if there's something to save, save it.

Bettors understandably plunged at Barbaro, sending off the undefeated Derby winner as the 1-2 favorite in the field of nine. Derby excuses were made for Sweetnorthernsaint and Brother Derek as the duo returned to try to quell the Barbaro storm.

Sweetnorthernsaint had slipped from bettors' minds since his Derby run. An outside post and his audacious middle move didn't help him in the first leg of the Triple Crown, and when trainer Mike Trombetta returned home and found nothing wrong with the gelding, he decided to come back and face Barbaro again.

Trainer Dan Hendricks put a line through Brother Derek's Derby after the colt lost a shoe, had an arcade trip around the first turn, and never got in the flow of the race. In the mile and a quarter race, he went a mile and a half. Like Trombetta,

The Kentucky Derby hero arrives at Pimlico

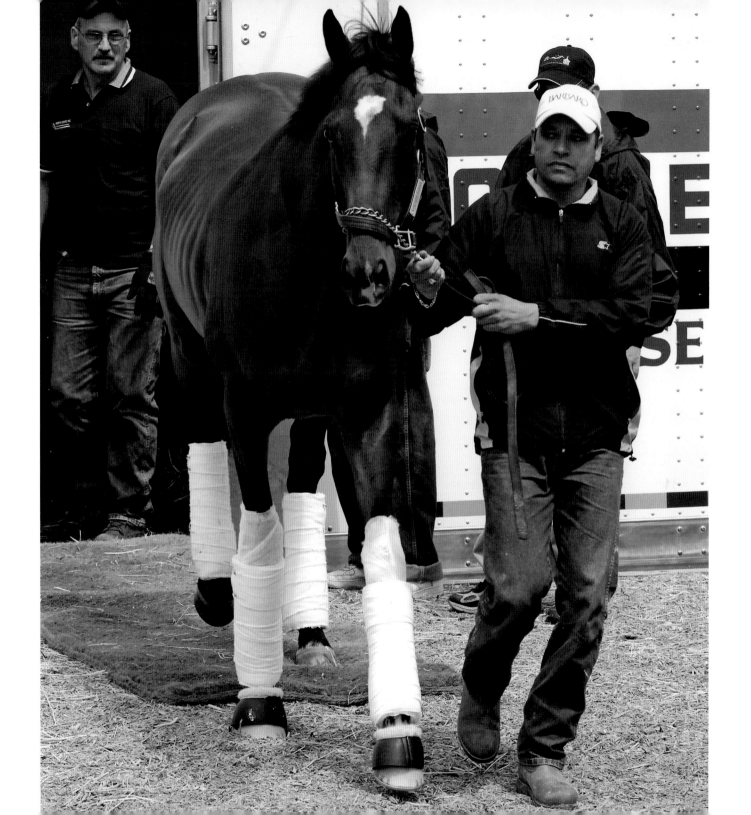

Hendricks couldn't find anything wrong since the Derby and lined up again, respectful of Barbaro but with eleven fewer horses with which to contend.

The only Triple Crown crasher who rated any kind of second look was Darley Stable's homebred Bernardini. Fresh off winning the Withers — but against just three rivals — the gorgeous son of A.P. Indy out of Breeders' Cup Distaff runner-up Cara Rafaela promised ability but lacked seasoning. He

Barbaro settles into the Derby winner's stall in the Pimlico stakes barn (opposite) and enjoys a bath

hadn't run as a two-year-old, broke his maiden in his second start (about a month after Barbaro won the Holy Bull for his fourth straight victory), and had never faced grade I horses, much less a horse such as Barbaro and in a race such as the Preakness. Bettors took a long look but still only made him fourth choice behind the Derby trio. Javier Castellano had the call for trainer Tom Albertrani.

"We knew he was a special horse, and after the Withers we felt this was a colt that we could take a chance on in the Preakness," Albertrani said. "I was quietly confident. We were very sure he would run well. As good as Barbaro was in the

Derby, we felt it was worth the risk to take him on. Maybe the Derby would take something out of him, and all the others coming out of it as well. We thought we were trying them at the right time."

Bernardini had always impressed Albertrani. Little things had kept the colt from making it to the races as a two-year-old, but once there Albertrani upped the ante with each start, going from maiden to Withers to Preakness. Bigger game had never fallen so easily.

The rest of the Preakness field appeared dwarfed by Barbaro. Hall of Famer Nick Zito entered the unproven Hemingway's Key. New York native Joe Lostritto came with longshot Platinum Couple. Fellow Fair Hill trainer Steve Klesaris brought overmatched Diabolical, who had been second to Barbaro in the Laurel Futurity in November. Kiaran McLaughlin had skipped the Derby with the speedy Like Now and aimed him for the Preakness. Greeley's Legacy, who was shut out of the Derby due to lack of earnings, arrived in hopes of picking up a check.

In keeping with tradition, all of the Preakness starters, except Brother Derek, were saddled on the Pimlico turf course. Hendricks opted for the tranquility — or at least solitude — of the Pimlico paddock, inside the grandstand, where his horse handled everything with aplomb.

Barbaro had acted up the past two times when Matz tightened his girth in preparation for a race. Nothing bad, just a pop and a hop before walking around the paddock. For the Preakness walk, Matz used a foam pad and girth designed to minimize the tightness of the racing girth. Matz had used the

Barbaro waits to be saddled for the Preakness

same apparatus in Barbaro's paddock schooling leading to the Derby. Matz saddled Barbaro without an anxious moment. The horse, multi-tasking like always, dove his head at the turf for a bite of grass. Gretchen Jackson, smiled, "He wants grass."

Matz snapped his head, "Don't even say that," and the Barbaro team laughed away all those days of wonderment about whether Barbaro was simply a good turf horse.

Prado made his way across the balcony of the Pimlico jocks' room and down the outside steps, across the track, and onto the turf, quietly confident, the way he had learned to be while dominating the rider colony so many years ago at Pimlico.

"When I saw him on the grass in the paddock, my mouth dropped. I said, 'Wow, look at this,' " Prado remembered. "The only concern was when I was riding earlier in the day. Pimlico was always a speed-favoring track, more packed down. But they added dirt, and it was a little more loose. But he had run at so many different racetracks, I thought he can handle it."

Prado's awe continued from the paddock to the post parade. It was a special moment for the jockey. Here he was, returning to his old stomping grounds, riding the best horse he'd ever ridden, moments away from the second leg of the Triple Crown. He couldn't help but look down at Barbaro, look out at the crowd, and anticipate what was about to happen. Barbaro showed his eagerness for the job at hand, playfully tossing his head and hopping up and down while waiting for post time.

"He was feeling very happy, excited to be there," Prado said. "Not at any point did he give me any doubts how he was going to run. He was looking good, feeling good, acting good."

Starter Bruce Wagner called for the horses, and Barbaro loaded comfortably, fourth of the nine starters. As the final horse, Diabolical, walked into the outside stall, Barbaro heard the latch of the back door lock and thought it was time to go. Barbaro broke through the gate, awkwardly clenching his body and scrambling through the metal doors and onto the open track. The magnetically held front doors of the starting gate are designed to open if hit firmly. It doesn't take a Herculean effort to bang them open, but it does take force. And it never bodes well.

Matz, sitting with his wife and family in the clubhouse terrace, gasped and looked on with concern. Just like in the Derby, the horse had left his hands; there was nothing he could do about it from here. But a feeling of dread consumed him.

Prado was gutted. In all his years, from Peru to Pimlico to Belmont Park, he couldn't recall riding a horse or seeing a horse break through the gate and win.

"Everything shut down for me," Prado said. "This can't happen. I thought, 'Well, if he doesn't run good today, this is why. But, look, he's a great horse and we'll live to fight another day.' "

In reality, it was the first time Barbaro had done anything out of character or without purpose during the whole magical tour he had taken everybody on since he started putting together inspiring breezes the previous spring at Fair Hill. Counted on for his class, his ease of motion, his constitution, Barbaro breaking through the gate was like hearing the Pope curse. Just out of place.

The Preakness jockeys make their way across the track to the turf course

Prado pulled up Barbaro in about fourteen strides, the horse gently shying from the outrider who had launched in gear to catch him. Prado jogged Barbaro back to the gate, trying to feel if something was wrong. State vet David Zipf checked him and deemed him sound. No harm done but an ominous sign nonetheless.

There was no time to contemplate any of this as the rest of the field waited in the gate. Barbaro loaded into stall six for the second time and the gates opened. He was a little less than two minutes away from adding to his legacy.

Barbaro broke a step slowly, and for the first time in his life he wasn't taking the race to his rivals. In all his other races, he had broken sharply and immediately gotten into the race. Even when he stumbled in the Derby, he was on the heat in strides, securing a perfect position. Amazingly, the horse had done it in every other race, like the racing gods had placed him down and then positioned the rest of the horses around him.

Not this time.

Outsider Go Now sprinted to the lead. Sweetnorthernsaint angled over from the outside and cleared Barbaro with ease. Newcomer Bernardini tucked into a perfect spot — Barbaro's spot — a stalking third, in the clear, at ease. Barbaro lagged in fifth as Diabolical outran him in the first sixteenth of a mile. He had never been off the bridle, even amongst the twenty-horse scramble in the Derby, in any race in his career. The Pimlico crowd and a million more watching the telecast struggled to find him in the field. Where was he? What was he doing there? What was going on?

"He wasn't there," Prado said. "When a couple of horses that don't have that kind of speed started going by him, I said, 'This isn't him. This isn't him.' He pulls and he wasn't

Barbaro is all composure in the post parade (opposite) then breaks prematurely from the starting gate

pulling. I felt like he wasn't there; no chance."

Prado searched for the answer as the Preakness, the Triple Crown, slipped from his grasp. Prado gave Barbaro a loose rein, niggled for a moment, and found nothing. No response. Within the first five strides, Prado realized the Barbaro he knew was gone. This wasn't him; the horse always broke like a rocket and could outrun anything into the first turn. Instead, he was struggling to keep up with Diabolical.

Prado hoped the ground was too heavy or maybe the horse had locked his stifle, a minor inconvenience compared to what was going wrong.

"I was thinking, 'forget about the race, forget about the

Triple Crown, forget about ...' I was hoping he was fine," Prado said. "You hear a lot of things, hooves clicking, who knows. The feeling was completely different."

Barbaro's action felt wrong and in an instant Prado was pulling him up.

What Prado was feeling was finally evident to the record crowd at Pimlico and the viewers at home as Barbaro's impotent stride separated him from the field. Analysis after analysis, it's impossible to detect the step that ended Barbaro's glorious run. But it happened, maybe somewhere between the eighth pole and the wire, or maybe it had already happened, somewhere, some place. Barbaro had broken down.

Prado jerked his body like he had snagged a tarpon off the Florida coast as Barbaro's three legs tried to staunch the pain of his fourth. Barbaro veered to the outside rail while Prado tried to halt the punishing steps that were blowing the colt's hind leg apart. Anyone watching could see the pain, the discomfort, the confusion as Barbaro threw his head trying to get away from Prado's grip. Every time Barbaro's right hind leg hit the dirt, he'd yank it up as if the dirt were scalding water. He managed to skip a beat, keeping his leg from touching down with every stride, but he was destroying his hind leg. Barbaro pulled up just past the wire and then miraculously skidded to the outside of the track. Outrider Sharon Greenberg was there instantly, blocking Barbaro from the field, which would quickly be returning down the stretch.

Prado wasn't a jockey any more but an emergency nurse

Barbaro fails to take hold of the bit in the early going

Prado pulls up the stricken Barbaro, dismounts, then bends over in disbelief

who was first at the scene of an accident, unknowingly reacting to disaster.

"Everything went blank; everything went zero. Like when you're on a plane and you look out the window and you see nothing but clouds," he said. "I was going with a lot of hopes, especially in Maryland, a lot of friends, a lot of fans, trying

to bring some joy, happiness, see a champion going through their state. Instead, all you got was sadness and tears. I was just hoping he didn't get put down. I felt bad for the people around him. My family was there; my kids were there. It was a very tough situation to swallow."

Prado jumped off and tried to hold Barbaro still as the colt writhed in desperation. Groom Rafael Orozco grabbed Barbaro, whose eyes blazed. Brette, watching the race from the inside paddock, ran to his stricken partner. Matz left his family and sprinted through the crowd in the second floor owner/trainer viewing area and was there in a flash. Prado's eleven-year-old daughter, Patricia, leapt from her mother

and ran toward the track, disappearing into the crowd. The Jacksons never hesitated, going straight to their horse. Track superintendent Jamie Richardson and his assistant, Glenn Kozak, hustled to the horse. The Maryland Jockey Club's Joe Miller scrambled off his chair at the head of the stretch and jumped into the track's horse ambulance, turning the key and preparing to floor it, knowing that he'd have to wait for the field to come past the second time but knowing time was critical.

Standing on the jocks' room balcony, Dr. Scott Palmer

Barbaro is comforted (opposite) as Bernardini streaks to victory

thinking how to diagnose Barbaro and police the situation. Palmer thought about rushing to the track but knew it wasn't his place. Once a vet, always a vet, Palmer watched, systematically diagnosing the injuries. Palmer knew it had to be more than a simple fracture.

"When I saw the leg flailing to the side coming down the track," Palmer said. "I knew it was life threatening."

Dr. Dan Dreyfuss, who's been doing Matz' veterinary work since he brought his first horse to Maryland, darted out of the hospitality tent at the stakes barn, scattering plastic chairs in his wake, and ran for his truck, the one with the crash box created for accidents like this.

Dreyfuss' partner, Dr. Nick Meittinis, watching from the grandstand, gasped like everyone else in the crowd and called Dreyfuss. The veterinary partners knew to divide and conquer, Dreyfuss was going to the track, so Meittinis sprinted to the

watched in disbelief as Matz, his childhood friend, ran down the track. Off duty from his equine practice in New Jersey, Palmer happened to be standing next to Dr. Larry Bramlage, the on-call vet for the American Association of Equine Practitioners, who was immediately in the firing line, already

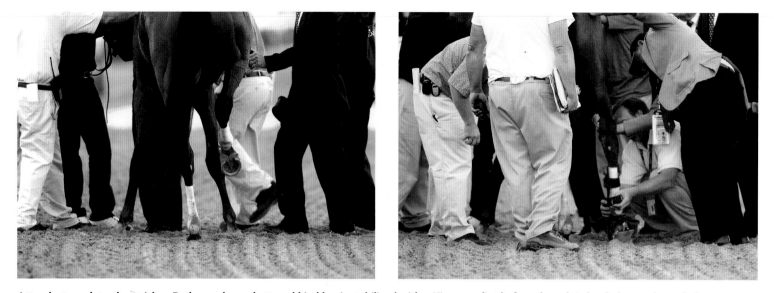

Attendants rush to the stricken Barbaro whose shattered hind leg is stabilized with a Kimzey splint before the colt is loaded onto the ambulance

stakes barn, thinking all the time — clear stall 40, get the digital X-ray machine, need a Robert Jones bandage, where's assistant Matt Hartman?

Prado's brother Jorge, who trains in Maryland, ran onto the track to try to help his brother. The Jockeys' Guild's Darrell Haire was there, consoling Prado.

The crowd finally understood. For a horse who had never lost, Barbaro was in for the fight of his life.

Darley Stable's Bernardini and jockey Javier Castellano crushed what was left of the Preakness field, drawing away from a spent Sweetnorthernsaint and a plodding Hemingway's Key. Castellano stood tall in his irons, punctuating the air with a right fist that brought along all the harshness of the sport.

Meanwhile, Dreyfuss couldn't get his truck through the crowd so he abandoned it and ran through the stable area, meeting up with Miller and Zipf at the quarter pole. Miller was already moving when Dreyfuss jumped on the side running board and yelled, "Go, go, go!"

Racetrack veterans, Miller, Dreyfuss, and Zipf had seen it before; they knew this was life threatening. It was a chilling ride to the end of the Pimlico stretch for three men who do their jobs because they love horses. They saw Barbaro as he tried to balance on three legs while people around him tried to keep him calm.

Dreyfuss got to the horse and was relieved to see that there was no blood. That had been his immediate concern. If it had been an open fracture, the horse would have been doomed. Dreyfuss could tell there were multiple breaks, but with the closed fractures there was a shot to save him. Dreyfuss knew Barbaro needed a Kimzey splint — an aluminum-splinted portable cast to stabilize the broken joint — immediately.

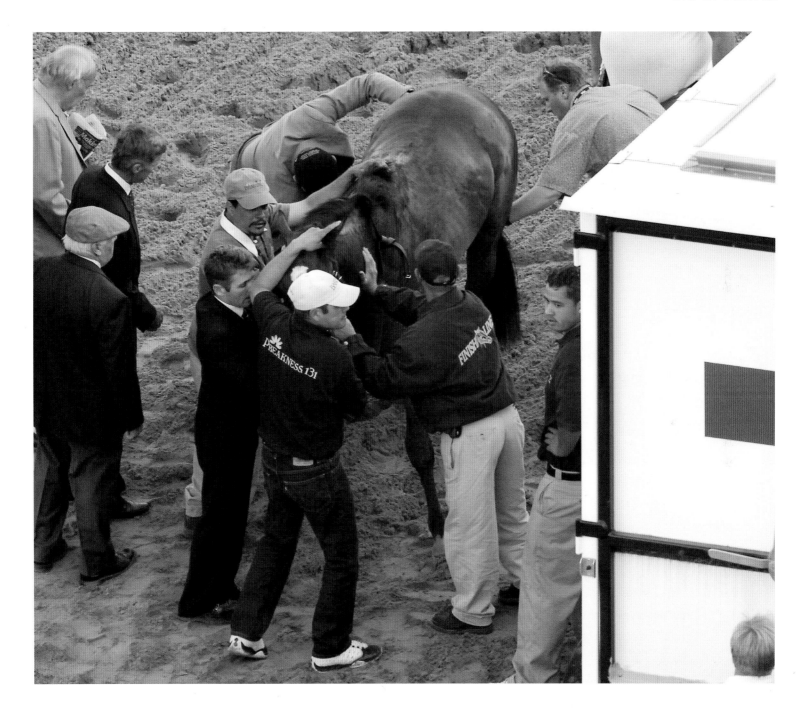

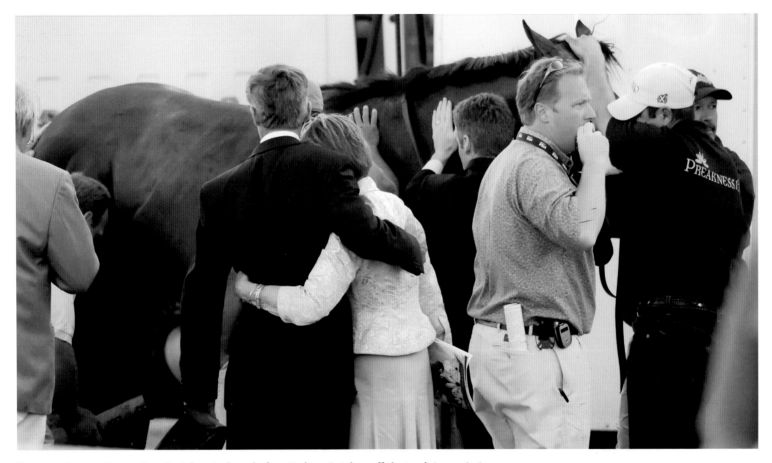

Matz comforts a disconsolate Gretchen Jackson before Barbaro is taken off the track (opposite)

Dreyfuss told Richardson to hold tight until he got his truck. Dreyfuss jumped in the human ambulance and went back for his truck.

Miller and other Maryland racing workers unfolded the screen, shielding the horse from viewers. The screen, a makeshift shroud of tarp about ten feet tall, usually means one thing — euthanasia. The fans, once jubilant, now dejected, immediately thought vets were pulling out a syringe to put down Barbaro on the spot. They booed at the insult.

"Don't you dare put this horse down," a woman yelled from the first floor seats.

Pressured to get the horse off the track, Richardson applied the Kimzey splint (Dreyfuss had given him lessons several years earlier) on Barbaro and then the assembled triage team helped Barbaro onto the ambulance. The horse was scared but manageable, his eyes wide from the searing pain.

A man's voice reverberated from the crowd — "Good luck, Barbaro." Then, almost as an afterthought, "You're going to need it, buddy." The man just stood there, dazed, eyes vacant, looking over the track. A woman next to him slumped in her chair, sobbing, as Miller maneuvered the horse ambulance down the racetrack.

Still thinking rationally, Matz called Palmer's cell phone and asked him to come back to the barn. Palmer took off in a sprint.

Dreyfuss met the ambulance on the way off the track and directed them to stall 40. Miller backed the ambulance under the stakes barn awning, getting as close as he dared to the stall.

A crowd collected around the stakes barn — reporters feeling more like intruders than writers, horsemen feeling more like accomplices than partners. The press asked the horsemen, "What do you think?" The horsemen, who had seen it before, didn't think there was a chance.

Dreyfuss stepped into the horse ambulance and administered the first medication Barbaro had received since Meittinis had given him a routine shot of Lasix, four hours before the Preakness.

Going on gut instinct — and twenty-plus years of practice — Dreyfuss looked over Barbaro, his size, his weight, his anxiety at that moment, and drew out enough Rompun, a short-term tranquilizer, and Torbugesic, a synthetic narcotic, to alleviate pain. He gave some in the muscle and some in the vein. Dreyfuss wanted to quiet the horse and soften the

pain but not enough to make him drowsy where he would lose coordination and further damage his leg or administer so much painkiller that the colt thought he could walk on his shattered leg. Within three minutes, the drugs hit Barbaro.

Miller and his team constructed screens to block any

The equine ambulance unloads its patient at the stakes barn

views, and the band of brothers steadied Barbaro and maneuvered him off the trailer, which had a ramp that could lower to nearly flush with the ground. Barbaro backed down the ramp, with Meittinis acting as a crutch for the broken leg and Dreyfuss holding the colt's tail to aid in balance, and turned about ninety degrees and hobbled into stall 40. Dreyfuss watched the colt balance on three legs, Barbaro putting his injured leg down once or twice in about thirty feet. He'd never seen a horse so adept at such a feat in such a dire situation. Dreyfuss was in awe of this horse, not that there was much time to think about awe or emotion or anything other than the next step in saving this horse.

Dreyfuss spoke to Bramlage on one of the racetrack radios, relaying what was going on so Bramlage could update NBC and try to subdue a delicate situation with the media.

The veterinarians positioned Barbaro near the right front corner of the stall and stood him diagonally so there was easy access to his hind leg from the front door. Dreyfuss administered a bit more tranquilizer, some non-steroidal anti-inflammatories and intravenous antibiotics, and set about diagnosing the injuries.

Palmer, Dreyfuss, and Meittinis weren't thinking about anything more than diagnosing the injury, stabilizing Barbaro, and getting him out of Pimlico as safely as possible. Whether he lived or died later wasn't their ultimate concern; they were there to give him every chance. To vets in the Mid-Atlantic region, it's a foregone conclusion that severely injured horses will go to the New Bolton Center. In cold reality, if New Bolton can't fix them, nobody can.

When the Jacksons arrived at the barn, they spoke to the vets and and then, as gracious as always, stepped back and got out of the way.

Dreyfuss never considered reaching for anything but painkillers, tranquilizers, and antibiotics from his truck.

"I worked on the assumption that we were going to try to save this horse. The thought never crossed my mind to even consider putting him down," Dreyfuss said. "That was not part of my thought process; when I saw it happen, it was the other direction; what can I do and what do I need to do to try and save this horse's life? It's not that you put it out of your mind and pretend it doesn't exist, but I was so focused on that one thing, that's what I did."

Dreyfuss continued to update Matz on what he was finding. Matz told him one thing, "Do everything you can to save him," and then let the doctors do their thing. Brette was in and out of the stall, suddenly an observer rather than a partner.

Groom Eduardo Hernandez stood in the corner, quietly comforting his comrade while the three vets crawled around Barbaro. The horse never moved, standing as still as the Trojan horse. Vets avoid anthropomorphizing their patients; it's just easier that way. Putting down a horse is hard enough without giving it human emotions and thoughts. But all three could see that this horse was basically saying, "OK, I'm hurt; you're trying to help. Fix me."

Hartman held the X-ray plate while Meittinis aimed the X-ray and Dreyfuss asked for the next view as he read the present one from a computer monitor. Each view encapsulated the entire injured region, from the coffin joint in the foot to halfway up the cannon bone. Right there on one frame, square in front of them, was the entire damage. To the vets it was not a diagnostic challenge to see that the leg was in pieces.

"No strut," Dreyfuss barked. "No strut."

It was the most editorializing done in that emotionless

stall that evening. Dreyfuss was searching for an intact piece of the bone that goes from the level of the fetlock joint down to the pastern joint, anything long enough where a surgeon could anchor the other pieces of bone. Barbaro didn't have that. Without it, the surgery becomes much more complicated and the prognosis much worse.

As Barbaro stood quietly, Dreyfuss, Meittinis, and Palmer flipped through the different views, getting an appreciation of just how catastrophic the injury was. Three breaks: a condylar fracture of the cannon bone; a break of the sesamoid bone in the ankle; and a comminuted — shattered — pastern bone. The pastern bone was in twenty pieces. The ankle was also dislocated. The condylar fracture had occurred first; the rest a chain reaction to the first piston out of place. God's ultimate joke when making species; man sprains an ankle or cracks a bone, he stops and hobbles off the field. The horse — a species of flight — sprains an ankle or cracks a bone and every step compounds the injury to the point of disintegration.

Dreyfuss continued to call out views until they had seen all there was to see. Barbaro's leg was still encased in the Kimzey splint, designed with aluminum so vets don't have to disturb the broken limb to X-ray an injury. Once they finished taking the X-rays, Dreyfuss removed the Kimzey splint and cut off Barbaro's run-down bandage to inspect the leg for cuts. Even a nick in the skin makes it an open fracture and further plummets the odds. Sometimes, in fractures like these, the bones break and damage the skin to the point where it loses its function as a protective layer. It's similar to an open fracture, even if the bones haven't broken through the skin. Dreyfuss crawled underneath Barbaro and searched the leg for even the smallest of cuts; he found the skin to be in relatively good shape. Obviously bruised but healthy, considering the trauma.

Once Dreyfuss deemed the skin to be in good shape, he gently cleaned the leg, preparing it for a modified Robert Jones bandage. Named for a World War I field surgeon, the bandage basically consists of a thick membrane of rolled cotton, gauze, and splints cut from six-inch PVC pipe that Dreyfus had cut for occasions such as these. The bandage goes on in layers, about three times the size of the horse's leg when finished. It's a temporary splint designed to immobilize the leg and to minimize the chances of the broken bones moving or breaking through the skin. It ran from the middle of Barbaro's gaskin to his hoof.

Palmer left the stall and told Matz the injury was about as bad as it could be. He told him the only shot the horse had was to do an internal fixation and the only guy who could pull it off was Dean Richardson at New Bolton Center. Every vet involved knew Richardson was Barbaro's only chance.

Matz and the Jacksons never hesitated, the decision unsaid — do what you can to get him to New Bolton.

The University of Pennsylvania's George D. Widener Hospital for Large Animals is world renowned. In racing and local equine lexicon, it's simply called New Bolton. With chief of surgery Dr. Dean Richardson, a recovery pool for horses after they wake up from anesthesia, and the cutting edge of veterinary science, there is no better place for an animal to go than New Bolton, whether it's a polar bear with a broken leg, a cow with a twisted intestine, or a Kentucky Derby winner with a pastern in twenty pieces.

Drs. Nick Meittinis (left), Dan Dreyfuss (center), and Larry Bramlage (right) address the media at Pimlico

Richardson had expertise in repairing the three fractures that afflicted Barbaro — but not on the same horse. "I had the confidence that would be the place to do it, with the sling, the recovery pool, and the whole thing. It seemed like a no brainer that that's what we needed to do," Palmer said. "The thought of putting him to sleep never came up in conversation; we never even discussed it. We said, 'Look, this is the only chance; this is what we've got to do to save this horse.' The Jacksons were very agreeable; they have a great relationship with New Bolton Center and Dr. Richardson."

Palmer called Richardson, who was in Loxahatchee, Florida, helping an old friend, Dr. Byron Reed, with two long, tiring surgeries. They finished the second one just in time to watch the Preakness on a six-inch television. Richardson sat down as a Barbaro fan; he got up as his surgeon. He knew before the phone rang that if the horse made it out of Pimlico, he was coming his way.

Dreyfuss, who had done his surgery residency under Richardson at New Bolton twenty years earlier, e-mailed the X-rays to Richardson. Richardson had read them within thirty minutes of when they were taken. Again, it wasn't a diagnostic challenge; a first-year vet student could diagnose Barbaro's fractures. Richardson prepared to return north to his home, his office, and the operating table at New Bolton Center.

The Jacksons offered to fly Richardson in their jet, but he declined, knowing there wasn't any hurry. Veterinary surgeons had learned the hard way that it was better for the horse to be stabilized — cooled out from the race, decompressed from the trauma and shock of the injury — before diving into surgery. Richardson also knew Barbaro would be in capable hands until he got there. Richardson booked a commercial flight for first thing the next morning.

Michelle Matz, Michael's daughter who works for him at Fair Hill Training Center, walked out of the barn and was quickly surrounded by reporters, none brave enough to ask a thing. She stopped and fought her tears. Writers, always sniffing for something, could only say they were sorry.

"It's not good," she said in disbelief. "It's not good."

Prado had retreated to the jocks' room, taken a shower, and changed into his street clothes. He hadn't heard any news about Barbaro. Prado had been around, so he prepared himself for the worst — that vets were putting down Barbaro at the very moment.

Prado didn't want to talk to the press, didn't want to talk to anybody. He was still in shock, hoping he was going to wake up from this nightmare.

"I couldn't believe what happened," Prado said. "I was just thinking, 'I just hope he's there. I hope when I get to the barn that I still see him.' I hope he's standing up and the people are working on him, instead of laying down."

Prado's valet had knocked the Pimlico sand from the jockey's red saddle, packed his tack bag, set out his clothes, and didn't utter a word. Prado mustered every bit of poise and resolve and made his way to the corner stall in the Pimlico stakes barn. The place where the connections of Smarty Jones, Funny Cide, Silver Charm, Real Quiet, and Charismatic had gathered and celebrated in years past. This time it was a MASH unit.

Barbaro was still standing; the skin wasn't broken; he was handling it ... that's about where the positives stopped. Digital X-rays were still being played and rewound, played and rewound on a monitor so all the views could be analyzed.

Nobody said anything as Prado gazed into the stall.

"When I saw him, I went from real down, real devastated, real broken-hearted to thinking, at least he's here, at least there's hope. That's the last thing you want to lose, hope," Prado said. "If he had 1 percent chance to survive, let's give it a try. Take the 1 percent and give it a try; let them work on it and see what happens. It was bad. It was … I don't know … very bad … you couldn't really speak."

Baltimore City Police readied for an escort to New Bolton Center, in Kennett Square, Pennsylvania, but located more in Unionville horse country, home of the Matzes, the Jacksons, and more than a few veterinary miracles. The nearly eighty-mile drive can be done in a little over an hour, without traffic. Track superintendent Jamie Richardson took the wheel of the horse ambulance with Kozak accompanying him. Miller and Hernandez manned the back, steadying and talking to Barbaro. Palmer and his wife, needing a ride to their car, jumped in the cab with Richardson and Kozak.

Brette scurried to his BMW sports utility vehicle, and Matz, coat and tie long since shed, jumped in shotgun and the two devastated horsemen followed the van out of the Pimlico stable area at 7:22 — an hour and three minutes since the Preakness field broke from the gate.

During the long drive Matz and Brette said fewer than twenty words to each other — things like "Do I turn here?"

Meittinis and Dreyfuss returned to the stall and started packing up equipment. The X-ray machine, digital processing machine, cotton roll wrappers, center rolls of elasticon, extra splints — the stall looked like a crash site.

Meittinis looked over at Dreyfuss, "What just happened here?"

Dreyfuss just shook his head and went to his truck to go scope a horse that had run poorly in the Preakness, all the while thinking Barbaro had a 10 percent chance of making it.

The van bumped along the wood-chip path, the same one on which Barbaro had walked like a rock star to the track just hours earlier and made a right on Northern Parkway, lights flashing, scattering Preakness-goers into the median and onto the shoulder. Palmer and his wife jumped out of the ambulance to find their car, left at an off-site parking lot so many hours ago

The caravan made a left on to 83 North, then the Baltimore Beltway, then I-95, passing beneath crowds that stood on overpasses from Baltimore to Port Deposit. Under Route 155, just before the Susquehanna River, the Valentin family braced from the wind gusts of passing cars, holding a handwritten sign in black magic marker that read, "God Bless Barbaro."

The family had sat down to watch the race and like all viewers, they had seen the impossible. It's strange what human nature will make you do. Learning that the horse was on his way to New Bolton, straight up I-95, they needed to do something proactive.

Maybe it was when Bramlage said, "Keep your fingers crossed … and say a prayer," on the NBC telecast that the Valentins dug around their house for a piece of poster board left over from a school project, found a pen, scrawled a message, and climbed into their Honda minivan, the one with the Havre de Grace Little League and God Bless the Troops magnets on the back, and drove to the closest overpass.

Joshua, eight, and Nickolas, six, held the sign in place, their fingers clutching it tightly while wind gusts from each

Baltimore City Police officers prepare to give the van carrying Barbaro an escort to the interstate

passing car buckled the corners of the handmade banner. Their mother, Elaine, stood behind them looking down I-95 while Isabella, ten months, slept in the backseat of the van.

"This is big horse country," Elaine said. "I grew up around horses and have a real soft spot for them. When they said it's going to be a race to save his life, that hits close to home. We

didn't know what else to do; we just felt like we needed to come out."

As the horse van headed north, Mike Gathagan, Maryland Jockey Club's director of communications, called New Bolton from his perch in the Pimlico press box. "We had 1,600 credentialed members of the press at Pimlico today.

And they're headed your way," Gathagan said, taking a deep breath and looking across a disheveled Pimlico press box.

Barbaro stood square and relaxed all the way to New Bolton. If there had been any hay in the hay net, he would have devoured it. Miller and Hernandez steadied Barbaro on the ride, all the while radioing to Kozak and Richardson to slow it down or speed it up.

"The horse seemed like he knew we were trying to help him," Miller said. "He was like, 'OK, you guys go ahead and do what you've got to do. I'm going to stand here and grin and bear it.' That's how he was on the track, how he was in the stall and on the ride up there, like, 'OK, let's go. You've got me; let's fix it.' All you could call it is class. Class."

Barbaro arrived at New Bolton just after nine where he walked fairly steadily, considering his right hind leg was shattered, into a stall in the hospital's intensive care unit. Kozak, Richardson, and Miller latched the ramp of the horse ambulance and with nothing left to do, turned around for the long, lonely trip back to Pimlico Racecourse.

The press set up in New Bolton's lobby, taking over the place. The local community began hanging handmade signs on the white fence at New Bolton's entrance.

"Godspeed Barbaro."

"Believe in Barbaro."

"God Bless Barbaro."

"We love you Barbaro."

Surgery was scheduled for 1 p.m. Sunday. Richardson had packed his bag and booked his flight. He'd be there in the morning.

Dr. Barbara Dallap, assistant professor of emergency medicine and critical care at New Bolton, inspected Barbaro and settled him into the intensive care unit for the night.

"He was very brave and well behaved under the situation and was comfortable overnight," Dallap said.

Palmer and his wife left New Bolton just before midnight, numb and dazed by everything that had happened. Palmer, just like Meittinis and Dreyfuss, knew he had helped sway the decision to try and save Barbaro.

"I thought he had a chance. I really thought he did or I wouldn't have put people through it, I wouldn't have put him through it. But I really thought it was worth a try," Palmer said. "As bad as it was, I think, most people would have recommended euthanasia. But it was because of who he was, who he represented. He deserved the opportunity to survive."

Palmer and his wife stopped at an Applebee's on Route 1, a few miles from New Bolton, before heading back to New Jersey. They ordered food, took a few bites, and stopped eating, frozen by the sight of Barbaro's torqued ankle on every news highlight on every overhead television. They paid the check and drove quietly home.

Twenty miles from New Bolton, the fluorescent lights in both of Matz' Fair Hill barns cut into the darkness. A solitary van driver from Brook Ledge deposited some traps — buckets, webbings, racing equipment — at the loading chute and drove away.

At the end of the long day, Barbaro's stall at the end of Matz' main barn stood empty. Two buckets full of water, deep straw banked up along the four walls, sliding door open. An empty stall at the end of a racing afternoon. Most of Matz' horses were asleep; a few rustled around like awakened giants. But the real giant wasn't coming back.

"He's still a coin toss."

———

— DR. DEAN RICHARDSON

A Coin Toss

The world awoke Sunday morning, dreading to hear bad news from New Bolton, though it felt inevitable. Richardson awoke, thinking about the radiographs he had seen on Saturday night and trying to piece Barbaro's leg together in his mind.

Barbaro had weathered Saturday night in relative comfort, his leg still splinted and immobilized in the same Robert Jones bandage put on by Dreyfuss and the other vets at Pimlico. Doctors reinforced the splint when Barbaro arrived at New Bolton to hold him over until surgery Sunday afternoon, but otherwise nothing else had been done to his leg. His temperature was normal; his heart rate back to where it belonged; his system functioning just as it should.

This was no longer the stressed-out horse last seen standing a few yards past the finish line at Pimlico, wired by adrenalin and pain. No, this was more like the Barbaro the world had come to expect, the one presiding over his barn at Fair Hill or looking over the training track ready for a gallop at Keeneland.

Barbaro ate dinner Saturday night and had managed to lie down in his stall, taking some weight off his leg and catching a little deep sleep. Although horses are able to sleep standing up, their deepest slumber comes when lying down, and Barbaro was able to maneuver well enough to lie down and get up again.

Sleep and appetite would play crucial roles in any chance of recovery, and at least for now he was eating and sleeping like a healthy horse.

Outside of Barbaro's peaceful confines, New Bolton had turned into Times Square. It became part vigil, part stakeout as Saturday night turned into Sunday morning, then Sunday afternoon, and finally Sunday night.

Richardson, having realized the seriousness of the injuries after examining the X-rays in Florida, arrived by noon on Sunday and was quickly confronted by the enormity of the situation.

"I was stressed. I was thinking about the operation a lot, thinking about exactly what I would do," Richardson said. "Obviously, I knew there was going to be press, but I figured I'd deal with that when the time came."

The time had come.

The press had taken over New Bolton. News vans were

double-parked in the front lot; reporters had camped out in the lobby; New Bolton's conference room was filled with media awaiting any word that could be relayed to the outside world. Realizing how much attention was focused on Barbaro's plight, Richardson decided — or was forced — to talk to the press before the surgery.

"I've never tackled one exactly like this," Richardson began.

"When will you begin the surgery?" a reporter asked.

"As soon as you stop asking me questions," Richardson said.

And so began Barbaro's remarkable surgery and Richardson's remarkable relationship with the press. Always confident and occasionally brash, Richardson knew it was easier to tell the truth than to remember lies so he told it straight from day one. Give Richardson a .44 Magnum and he'd be Dirty Harry Callahan, steadily doing it his way and not worrying about the critics. Give him a classroom of students or an operating table and he's Dr. Dean Richardson, chief of surgery at New Bolton Center, the best in the business.

Richardson would operate on the broken leg of a Kentucky Derby winner the same way he would on an Amish carthorse from nearby Lancaster County. That's the nature of his job. Born in Hawaii, Richardson went to Dartmouth College, originally wanting to be an actor until he realized he wasn't very good at acting. A horseback riding class changed his life's trajectory, and he went to vet school at The Ohio State, eventually becoming chief of surgery at New Bolton.

Chief of surgery at New Bolton is more than a diploma to hang on the wall; it means when the Derby winner shatters his leg, you're the first call. The only call. If Dr. Dean Richardson can't do it, no one can. Barbaro's life was literally in Richardson's hands, no one else's. Sure, he had a premier team assisting, but, ultimately, the decisions sat in his lap. He would try to combine medicine and horsemanship.

Richardson had repaired each separate break in past surgeries on other horses but he had never performed the kind of triple-pronged operation that Barbaro's leg would require. Nor was he aware of a similar case, leaving him without a reference. For the most part, Richardson knew after reading Barbaro's X-rays in Florida what he was going to do and how he was going to do it. He just hoped the surgery would go as close to what he expected. They rarely do.

After his ten-minute initiation with the press, Richardson departed, leaving reporters to call their editors and television crews to start rolling tape, and walked to the intensive care unit to begin prepping for the biggest surgery he had ever done. Biggest, in terms of exposure, nothing more. All surgeries mean the same thing to a surgeon.

Fitted into a sling that cradled him around the belly, chest, and hindquarters, Barbaro was anesthetized and lowered onto the operating table. Drs. Bernd Driessen and Lin Klein, and anesthesia resident Dr. Francesco Staffieri; anesthesia nurse Shannon Harper; and residents Drs. Liberty Getman, Steve Zedler, and David Levine began playing their specific roles in the surgery.

The presence of three breaks made the surgery unusually complex. Piling a long condylar fracture on top of an extremely unstable fetlock on top of a shattered pastern was the crux of the problem. Fixing a condylar fracture in the cannon bone is relatively easy. Repairing a shattered pastern has been done often, even pasterns that have been pulverized more

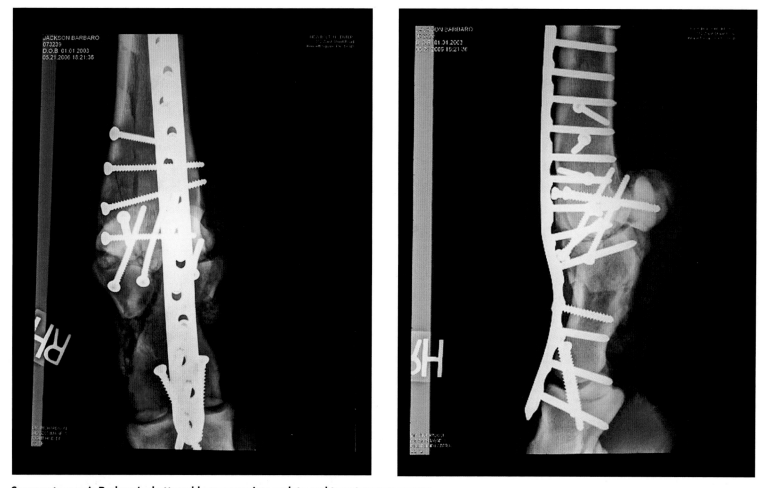

Surgery to repair Barbaro's shattered bones requires a plate and twenty-seven screws

severely than Barbaro's. The broken sesamoid, by itself, could have been managed. But in simple terms, to fix the pastern Richardson needed a secure cannon bone and fetlock joint. To fix the cannon bone, he needed a secure column of bone below it … three broken bones on top of each other made it difficult because there was nothing secure to hold the other insecure parts. That was the paramount problem. Think of it like LEGO bricks: the more pieces you try to connect end to end, the more precarious the structure becomes, never mind if the three pieces are fractured.

Because the leg was so badly out of alignment and the surgery so complicated, Richardson needed to open the horse's leg from hock to hoof. In surgeries possibly requiring two joints to be fused, it's best to open the leg and then start to piece the leg back together.

Richardson took a long look at the damage.

"I had seen the radiographs, and it looked exactly like what you expected it to look like," Richardson said. "You do get surprises in surgery; it happens commonly, but this time the radiographs pretty much told the truth. It wasn't pretty."

Richardson began putting together the jigsaw puzzle that had once been Barbaro's perfectly designed leg.

Richardson knew he had one huge decision to make. It centered on how he would address the pastern, the area that connects the fetlock to the hoof. It's made up of two bones: the proximal phalanx (long pastern bone), which Barbaro had shattered, and the middle phalanx (short pastern bone). By stopping the plate at the bottom of the long pastern bone, Richardson would have only fused the fetlock, which would certainly help Barbaro's future mobility, but it wouldn't be as sturdy.

The decision could only be made after opening the leg and looking inside. The fewer decisions during surgery, the better, but this was a big one.

Because Barbaro had shattered the long pastern bone so badly, Richardson was forced to go to the next secure piece of bone — the short pastern bone — as an anchor for the lower part of the plate, thus fusing the second joint in Barbaro's leg, the one between the long pastern bone and the short pastern bone.

To fuse both joints, Richardson removed all the cartilage — about three handfuls — from Barbaro's joints and then pieced together all the major fragments of bone to form a makeshift column. It would serve as the strut that Dreyfuss so desperately searched for at the stakes barn. Once this column was reconstructed, Richardson was able to put the locking plate into place, securing it with screws in an attempt to fuse the leg into one solid stilt. Because of the number of breaks and the amount of damage in the leg, a bone graft was taken from the tip of Barbaro's hip to use in the leg. With antibiotics impregnated into the bone graft, those pieces were put into place where more bone was needed. After that, extra screws were inserted to secure the other fragments outside the plate. All of these procedures were done in a certain sequence, learned through years of practice, and once finished a fiberglass cast was put on Barbaro's leg. The surgery lasted six hours.

Richardson and his team knew the easy part was over; now everything would hinge on how Barbaro woke up from the anesthesia. New Bolton uses a special pool recovery system where a monorail transports the horse, suspended from a sling, from the operating room to a recovery pool. The horse is lowered into a floating rubber raft, with his legs hanging down into rubber boots, like fishermen's waders. This way the horse wakes up and fights against water, nothing else.

New Bolton's system is as good as it gets in veterinary surgery. Still, it's a stressful time, especially for Barbaro, who had been under anesthesia for six hours. Horses are followers; they don't process information like humans and they weigh 1,200 pounds. They can react violently when coming out of anesthesia, risking reinjury or worse.

"I was pretty sure we were going to be able to get to the point where the horse was in the pool, waking up," Richardson said. "You never are sure after that; you never know what the

Barbaro's supporters show their concern with cards, flowers, and carrots

horse is going to do waking up; you never know if they're going to be a nitwit or a good horse. It's a scary time."

Barbaro started to come to in the pool and, as always, was anything but a nitwit. Once fully awake in the pool, Barbaro was blindfolded and hoisted out of the water and delivered to a padded recovery stall where he stood up immediately. Actually, he thrashed around rambunctiously but then settled down without a problem. The colt was comfortable but still a long, long way from home.

All this time, the lobby at New Bolton was roiling with press. Dr. Corinne Sweeney, Widener Hospital executive director and associate dean for New Bolton, had the unenviable task of communicating with the press. But there was nothing new to communicate — the horse was still in surgery. Sweeney tried her best to placate the press, but there wasn't a nugget of information to be mined during the eight hours of waiting.

Flights were booked, canceled, and booked again, all

with a certain pall. "Of course, it could all be academic," one writer told her editor, "if he … if he doesn't make it."

Dunkin' Donuts boxes were replaced with Domino's Pizza boxes. Sixteen pizzas were devoured in minutes. Sunday papers, from the *Philadelphia Inquirer* to the *New York Times*, sat in piles. One with an above-the-fold color picture of Barbaro, running with his foot grotesquely torqued into oblivion.

A publication titled "On Any Given Day — a day in the life of New Bolton Center" sat on a counter. They'd want to rewrite that after this epic day. Mobile phones charged in the few open sockets. Laptop computers hung off desks, sat on the floor, nestled in every nook and cranny, all with stories in limbo. Writers on deadline had their stories written; they just awaited word on whether they could finish it with — the horse is stable or the horse is dead.

Red roses, flower arrangements, also filled the room — one with a card for Barbaro Jackson and another one addressed to Barbara Jackson, yep Barbara; the florist obviously wasn't watching the Preakness. Carrots piled up. The Coke machine rumbled in constant demand. Baseball updates came in: the Phillies led the Red Sox. Fox 29, News 10, 2 Action News, Storm Tracker 6 vans idled in the parking lot. "This horse has been in surgery for seven hours," was said in exasperation. It felt like waiting around for someone to die.

On the walls of the lobby, among the roster of New Bolton donors, their names in steel, were those connected to Matz and Barbaro: Mrs. Helen K. Groves, Matz' mother-in-law; Ms. Helen Alexander, his sister-in-law; Kleberg Foundation; Mr.

Dr. Dean Richardson addresses the media after Barbaro's surgery

and Mrs. F. Eugene Dixon Jr.; Mrs. J. Maxwell Moran. Matz' owners, his in-laws, his family helped make New Bolton what it is today. Now, New Bolton was here to repay the favor.

Matz had been called at his home with the news as Barbaro was coming out of surgery. He numbly turned left out his driveway on to Route 82, the country road, past Blow Horn Mill (where the sight line is so hidden drivers blow their horn to warn oncoming traffic) and to New Bolton. The trip took less than ten minutes but felt like ten years. Once Matz was there, Richardson briefed him on the surgery, about the decent blood supply to the injury, about the most crucial stage — three to seven days after the surgery — when infection can take over. Both men were gassed by the stress of trying to save a horse's life.

At 8:55 Sunday night, Matz and Richardson appeared in the hallway leading to the lobby. Laughing. At least he's alive was the only thing an observer could deduce. The two tried-and-true horsemen ducked into an office at the end of the hall before facing the firing line that awaited.

Richardson and Matz took the stage and then told the hard, cold truth. The horse handled the surgery, woke up from anesthesia, and was resting comfortably in the stall. But all that was grade-school field day compared to the Ironman Triathlon that lay ahead. Infection, laminitis, colic, failed fusion, diarrhea. Just like John Stephens said when the horse left Ocala as a two-year-old, put a horse in a rubber stall and he'll die of a rubber allergy. Well, put in a locking plate, twenty-seven screws, and fuse two joints in a horse's leg and everyday hurdles become walls.

"At this very moment he's extremely comfortable in the leg," Richardson said. "He practically jogged back to his stall.

He pulled us back to his stall. Right now, he's very happy. He's eating. Things right now are good, but I've been doing this too long to know that day one is not the end of it."

Richardson knew this was far from a success story. He knew he could complete the surgery; that was what he had learned in vet school and what he had honed in twenty-five years of surgery at New Bolton. Equine surgery to the laymen is unfathomable. Equine surgery to Richardson is his job. It's what he does.

Richardson and Matz spoke to the press while cameras clicked and reporters talked over each other to try and get their questions answered. Some got the word and sprinted, dialing their editors in haste to say, "run version one, run version one, the horse is stable." Matz' steely blue eyes were glassy. He stared blankly into the crowd. He wanted to be anywhere but here, talking about his horse who was in a recovery stall, trying to shake off the haze of six hours of anesthesia, twenty-seven hours of stress, and one bad step.

Richardson was deadly serious but naturally punchy after piecing together the jigsaw puzzle inside Barbaro's leg. Five words he uttered made the biggest impression: "He's still a coin toss," Richardson said, like always, straight and true.

Exhausted but optimistic, Matz joins Richardson in a press conference

That phrase would become the surgeon's mantra.

"The surgery was very, very difficult," Richardson said. "We were able to get the appropriate metal implants in the leg to hopefully fuse his fetlock joint and stabilize the limb to the point where he'll be able to be salvaged as a stallion. The most important thing to emphasize, before anybody asks the question, is this is just the absolute first step in any case like this."

Richardson adamantly tried to drive home the point that this horse wasn't cured. Forget about when he was going to be discharged; forget about whether he could one day mount a mare. The surgery was like putting on crampons before tackling Everest. When you deal with the types of catastrophic injuries that Richardson deals with daily, you learn reality or you learn another trade. When Richardson said it was a coin toss, it wasn't a coin toss that he could put the leg back together; it was a coin toss whether the horse would be hit with complications that would kill him. The complications, as Richardson knew, were multiple and formidable.

As Matz fled the building, he was asked about his gut instinct.

"I don't know. I sure was happier when I saw him standing there," Matz said as he walked to his car in the empty parking lot behind New Bolton.

Team Barbaro

Michael Matz has a way of minimizing his words that maximize the meaning — "One minute I had the best three-year-old in the country; the next minute we're trying to save the best three-year-old in the country's life."

Whether Barbaro would survive that mission couldn't be determined right after the surgery, no matter how smoothly things had gone. Richardson knows, far too well, to keep a lid on any exuberance he feels when a horse gets out of surgery. It's the weeks and months after surgery that carry the brunt of risk. Complications lurk everywhere. Barbaro would be day to day for months and months. Richardson could not stress that enough.

The balance between modern science and inherent equine fragility was guaranteed to ebb and flow as Barbaro's leg healed and his body fought off the next round of obstacles.

Barbaro's followers yearned for any positive signs that he would prevail. They followed his progress on the University of Pennsylvania's Web site, which had more than 177,000 hits immediately after the surgery. An anonymous donor plunked down a deposit to start the "Barbaro Fund," not for Barbaro's care, but for work done at New Bolton. Handmade signs multiplied on the front gate of New Bolton. Carrots, mints, flowers arrived by the truckload.

Each morning brought a little more hope; Barbaro had survived another night, gaining a little more ground in his journey from that fateful day at Pimlico.

Each day also brought worry to Richardson, the Jacksons, Matz, and anybody else familiar with all the things that could possibly go wrong.

Winning and surviving had switched places. Matz had made so many precise decisions with Barbaro, resulting in a Derby victory. Now, Richardson was making those decisions and they had nothing to do with winning races: nutrition, medication, schedule for cast changes, supportive shoes for both hind feet. The decisions were endless.

Richardson obviously focused on Barbaro's broken right hind leg, but he also concentrated on Barbaro's feet. They were key to the colt's recovery, especially the left hind foot that was bearing the brunt of the weight and was in constant risk of laminitis. All four racing plates had been pulled before surgery and a special glue-on shoe had been put on Barbaro's right hind foot. Five days after the surgery, he was fitted with a special three-part glue-on shoe on his left hind foot to try and reduce the risk of laminitis.

Barbaro was bedded down in a twelve-by-thirteen-foot stall in the intensive care unit at New Bolton. He was eating well, the same sweet feed he ate as a racehorse, and all his vital signs looked good. He devoured alfalfa (for the calcium) and relished the fresh-cut grass brought to him by Gretchen Jackson on her daily (and sometimes twice-daily) visits.

Equine medicine isn't any different than human science. The fitter and more athletic, the better attitude a patient has, the more likely the chances of recovery. The qualities that made Barbaro an exceptional racehorse were helping him be an exceptional patient at New Bolton.

"He actually is so far a very good patient," Richardson said a few days after the surgery. "His mental attitude is great. He's a very active, inquisitive, bright type of a horse. He's a perfect three-year-old colt."

Matz trained his horses at Fair Hill and then stopped at New Bolton on his way home every day. The half-hour drive would become a ritual. Usually the last one to leave the barn, Matz would walk to his Volvo station wagon, set his briefcase inside, and pull out of the parking lot and head down the dusty Fair Hill driveway. He'd check his messages that had piled up during the morning, make a call before heading into the dip past Barbaro's vet Kathy Anderson's house, where phone reception is lost among the Pennsylvania hills. Then back up, usually on his phone again, through what used to be hunt country, past the urban sprawl, back into the country, before arriving at New Bolton. Then he'd shimmy into hospital scrubs and make the tepid walk to Barbaro's stall in the intensive care unit. A journey he would make methodically every day

for … he didn't want to think about where it would end.

And every day his old friend Barbaro would greet him with his ears pricked, inquisitive about what was going on. The horse had simply switched his verve for racing to a verve for visitors. If he had an off day, he didn't let Matz see it.

"The progress was slow, but we felt he was going to come through," Matz said. "We never doubted he was going to come through."

Matz or Brette would change Barbaro's bandages every day; they'd tie him by his halter to the back wall and rub him down with brushes and a rub rag. Just fool with him like he was going out in the next set. They knew him; he knew them. It was good for both men and horse. Despite a broken leg, he was still a big, strong three-year-old colt with a lot of life left in him.

That's the part that stings. Barbaro was different. Matz primped him to arrive at the Derby as a fresh, sound, sky's-the-limit horse. His Derby was other-worldly, the way he came down the stretch, pouring it on while Prado sat. Just sat, scoffing at the hopelessness behind him, enjoying the moment. The power. No horse had bullets like Barbaro. Look, you can stand at the rail of most tracks and say, that one will break down, that one will never make it, that one is ouchy, find a new job for that one. Watching Barbaro was watching the untouchable.

"He gave me six good races, and I'm sure he was trying to give me seven," Matz said a few days after the Preakness. "It was waiting for this race, waiting for this race and then it's over in thirty seconds. You don't realize what you had until you don't have it any more. Maybe you'll never get it again."

Matz, still composed and steady, looked tired, four days

after the Preakness. His steely blue eyes had changed to simply tired blue eyes. Handmade cards sat in piles on his desk in his tack room at Fair Hill.

Had the trainer won the Preakness, the world would have followed him. Barbaro having broken down in the Preakness, the world joined him.

"I just thought he was going to win the Triple Crown," Matz said. "Racing needed it, and I thought he was the horse to do it. I'm better when I don't talk about him, when I just go and try to look for another one but I know there isn't going to be another one, maybe ever, as good as he was. It's not so much sinking in that I won the Derby but more that I lost a good horse. That's what is sinking in."

Matz had a vet inject Barbaro's hocks before the Florida Derby; that was the only non-routine procedure he could recall the horse needing in his career. In racing, injecting a horse's hocks is about as routine as a flu shot.

"He never had a bad work; he never had a … he never had anything wrong. I don't remember him ever being lame," Matz said. "This horse is so strong — it's unbelievable how strong he is — every picture we saw of him, all four legs were off the ground, the power. He would have been a better four-year-old than a three-year-old. There was no telling how good this horse could have been. He was a trainer's dream; he just wanted to do it."

Maybe that's what could get Barbaro through this. The want. That's all there was to hold on to at this point: his desire to fight and New Bolton's ability to keep him alive.

After the Preakness, Prado thought about taking some

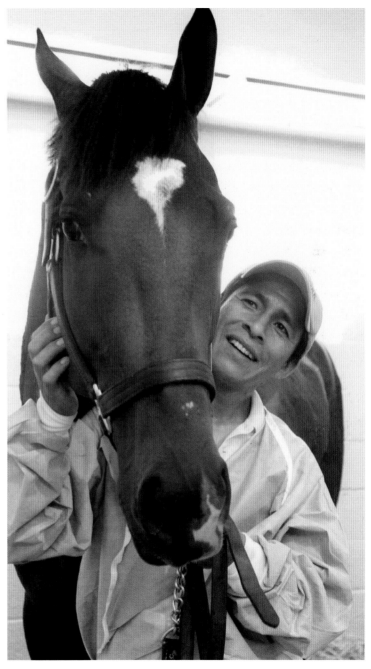

Edgar Prado visits his good friend Barbaro at New Bolton

Thousands of fans sign the world's largest get-well card at Belmont Park on Belmont Stakes day

yelled at Prado — "You screwed up. You broke down Barbaro. You should quit. Go home."

Prado never looked up.

"You always find good people, you always find bad people, and you always find ignorant people. That's everywhere," Prado said. "But, I really wanted to take time off."

After racing on Sunday, Prado hopped on a plane and flew to Florida to be with his family. He spent two days in Florida, clinging to the Internet and the television, still searching for news about Barbaro. Finally, he realized he needed to set the record straight. Instead of formulating uneducated theories on what had happened, the world should

time off, maybe going back to Peru for a respite from the storm. He retreated to his New York home, turned his phone off, thought about his mother, thought about Barbaro, thought about quitting.

"First, my mother passed away; that was a very tough situation. You go from so down then so high when I won the Derby and now I'm back again," Prado said. "I thought about taking some time off, but giving up is for quitters. 'No, I'm going to go back and ride.' The busier I stay, the better it is. Then I won't have time to think about the whole situation."

Prado returned to Belmont, where he was harshly reminded.

Hecklers hung over the railing near the paddock and

hear from Prado.

"It was good to let people know what really happened," Prado said. "People started making their own opinions, saying something was wrong with the horse. I decided it was better to talk to the press. Athletes get hurt. It's not the only sport that the athletes get hurt. I explained that to the media; there was a little release."

Prado returned to New York, rode for two days, and then made his way to New Bolton on May 30, nine days after the surgery.

Seeing his friend made it better. Barbaro had never been mean, but he had always had a mind of his own, an iron constitution about pretty much everything, knowing what he

wanted and when he wanted it. That hadn't changed.

"I felt a lot better when I saw him. It seemed like Barbaro and the people working with him had a good communication," Prado said. "He handled it. He knew he was in trouble. He did everything he was supposed to do. It was like somebody talked to him, 'You're going to be in this splint today. When we take it off, you can lie down.' Like he was reading."

There was plenty to read. The Associated Press, Reuters, the *New York Times*, the *Wall Street Journal*, the *Los Angeles Times*, *Forbes*, the *Baltimore Sun*, the *International Herald Tribune*, *USA Today*, and other newspapers covered Barbaro like a presidential election. Matz had received 130 e-mails by Tuesday after the Preakness. Goswell at Fair Hill had two hundred e-mails clogging her inbox. New Bolton was another story — they were being bombarded with phone calls, e-mails, swarming media attention from CNN to NPR, Pennsylvania's *Daily Local News* to the Associated Press.

On June 13, three days after Jazil won what was supposed to be Barbaro's Belmont Stakes, Richardson changed the cast on Barbaro's right hind leg for the first time while the horse was under general anesthesia. Richardson took radiographs of the leg and could see the bone opacifying, or taking, which is the first positive step in the fusion. The plate and screws hadn't budged, and everything was on par with what Richardson had hoped.

Richardson had turned into superhero, ducking and jiving against the odds while taking care of Barbaro, dealing with the suffocating press attention and his other duties as chief of surgery at New Bolton. In Richardson's twenty-seven

Well-wishers left banners and signs at the New Bolton entrance

years of operating on horses at New Bolton, this was the most watched case he had ever done. The horse occupied his time at New Bolton and every ounce of mental energy when he left. Yeah, he'll admit he was stressed, but don't pity him.

"To me, it's not a matter of life and death. To the horse, it is. The reality is that it's my job. If I'm not going to do it, who's going to do it?" Richardson said. "That's why I am at the New Bolton Center, why I'm the head of the Widener University. I could be making a lot more money doing simple surgery all the time, but the reasons I like my job are — one, I love to teach; two, I enjoy doing real basic research; and, three, I like to be in a place where I have the opportunity to deal with the hardest types of cases."

As June turned to July, the Barbaro case hummed along, almost lulling Richardson into believing the horse would glide through the medical journal, page by page, without being hit by any of the villains loitering inside.

"Despite your knowledge about the situation, despite what you know, you can't help but get more optimistic," Richardson said. "Every day you go in there and the horse looks great, but the facts are facts and bad things can still happen."

In early July, Barbaro's temperature rose slightly and he started getting uncomfortable in his hind legs. On July 3, Richardson changed the cast for the second time, replacing two bent screws and adding three new ones across the pastern joint for additional support. These screws bridged the pastern joint and were not part of the original fracture repair. The bent screws didn't surprise Richardson because Barbaro had been active in his cast. Richardson was happy with the results of the radiographs: The leg was still healing.

Barbaro recovered from anesthesia without incident in the pool.

Two days later, Barbaro was still uncomfortable, forcing Richardson to change the cast again. He also treated a small

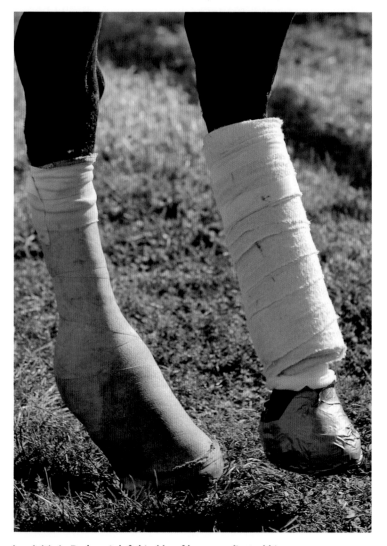

Laminitis in Barbaro's left hind hoof has complicated his recovery

abscess on his left hind foot that caused concern; anything wrong in that foot sent up the red flag of laminitis.

"He wasn't comfortable with the second cast, so we decided it would be best to replace it sooner rather than later," Richardson said.

The week would continue to bring bad news to the Barbaro camp. New radiographs had shown progressive bone healing, a very positive sign, but a new infection appeared in his right hind leg, forcing Richardson to operate on Barbaro for the third time in five days. Richardson removed the plate that was securing his pastern, replaced it with two smaller plates, and thoroughly cleaned the site of infection. It was nearly twenty hours of surgery. Here was Barbaro, six weeks after the Preakness undergoing a surgery three times as long and just as precarious as the first operation. Progress? Hardly. Richardson fitted him with a longer, more supportive cast.

Worst of all, Barbaro was developing laminitis.

"The third anesthesia, which was right around the time he foundered, that was the one time he had a very, very bad time in the pool," Richardson said. "We were in the operating room or the recovery room for sixteen hours; that was very tiring. Beyond exhausting."

Laminitis is the equine grim reaper, hiding in the dark. This painful condition, also known as founder, has any number of causes, including excessive weight-bearing in one limb. It occurs when laminae, the strong connecting tissues that attach the pedal (coffin) bone to the inner hoof wall, are inflamed, causing the coffin bone to rotate or sink away from the hoof wall. Think of putting so much pressure on your thumb, your thumbnail separates from your thumb, but a thousand times more complex.

Barbaro foundered quickly and radically. Nearly his whole hoof sloughed off, which in turn rapidly increased the chances of overloading the right leg, which had basically been torn apart and put back together with new hardware. With a foundered left foot and an infection and new plate in his right pastern, Barbaro didn't have a good hind leg to stand on. Everything was unraveling.

"His laminitis happened so quickly and so severely, it was very, very rapidly worsening laminitis to the point where his foot was basically falling off," Richardson said. "I kept getting letters, e-mails, and phone messages from all these people, well meaning, but they all think I'm trying to treat a garden variety of laminitis. They have their suggestions; things are meaningless when you talk about a horse whose hoof has literally been removed."

On July 9, local bloodstock agency Walnut Green held a cocktail party awarding Pennsylvania Governor Ed Rendell with a man-of-the-year award for helping to usher in the slots in Pennsylvania. Richardson, a member of Walnut Green's advisory board, was there chatting with trainers whom he'd done work for in the past and catching up with some veterinary colleagues. Mostly, he was acting. Richardson had finished twenty hours of surgery on Barbaro and knew the horse was in deep water. The surgeon was local celebrity by then, and everybody wanted a piece of him that night, just to ask him about Barbaro, pat him on the back for saving the Derby winner.

"We were really struggling, but with this job you have to suck it up. It's not like I'm going to hide because things are going badly. We tried to let people know an honest appraisal of the horse's condition," Richardson said. "I wasn't fixated on feeling sorry for myself. I felt sorry for Barbaro. In this job you're worried about the patient."

The next day Richardson replaced Barbaro's cast again, his sixth, with a shorter one and continued to battle the laminitis. The long cast had provided extra support in the anesthetic recovery phase, but the shorter one gave him more mobility. All this was done under mild sedation and in a sling.

Prado and Matz, ever professionals, prepared to go to Saratoga for six weeks at the end of July. Prado asked a few confidants about laminitis. They painted a bleak picture, so Prado made one final trip to New Bolton before going to Saratoga. Prado and his wife left their New York home at three in the morning and headed south. Prado knew the way.

Prado spent about two hours with the horse, just hanging out with an old friend. It went unsaid that it might be goodbye.

"The people at New Bolton put a lot of work into it [taking care of Barbaro], but most importantly, they put a lot of love into it," Prado said. "It's unbelievable that he brought so many people together. He earned the hearts of a lot of people. He did that. Nobody else."

Richardson and his team were doing everything they knew to manage the pain and discomfort, but Barbaro was less and less comfortable. The laminitis had forced him to alter his weight from his left leg to his right and it had also elevated his pulse. Richardson used a sling to alleviate some of the burden and epidurals to control the pain. The horse was in for another long, hard battle.

Barbaro's hoof was barely attached to his coffin bone,

causing short-term discomfort and long-term concerns. Walking becomes agonizing for a horse with laminitis as the hoof is literally separated from the bone inside. Barbaro wasn't writhing in pain — he was eating, drinking, moving around his stall, getting up and down, but the question was could they manage his comfort for the long, slow process of growing his hoof enough where he could walk on it. A rapid recovery for his type of laminitis would be six months.

"The severity was shocking," Richardson said. "It made me physically ill. I know it's a cliché, but I wanted to puke it was so bad. And we had so much farther to go. We knew at that point, we were nowhere close for him to bear weight on his other leg. That's what made it tough."

Team meeting.

Richardson, if pressed, thought Barbaro's chances were less than 10 percent, maybe less than 5 percent when he met the Jacksons and Matzes at New Bolton to decide whether they should go on. The crew-cut surgeon, the former Olympian, his wife — a lifelong horsewoman — the baseball man, and the girl who fell in love with horses were trying to decide the fate of the greatest horse they'd ever known.

Roy Jackson was the first one to cry.

The conversation alternated between talking and crying, trying to decide what to do. Tears flowed, opinions shared … all with Barbaro looking out the stall door.

"We were like that [close]; at least I was, [to not] putting him through any more hoops when he got the laminitis. I was really upset; is this fair?" Gretchen Jackson said. "It was pretty dire straits there … we all agreed because there's Barbaro, looking out his stall door, saying, 'Hey, can't I vote, too? I want to be given every chance.' "

Matz finally said his peace.

"Look, you've got to give him a chance, give him a chance for at least ten days or two weeks. If it doesn't work by then, then go ahead and put him down," Matz recalled telling the others. "That's my feeling; you've got to give him at least ten days to two weeks, and that's the way it is. Two weeks led to two months and on, and here he is."

"At the end there was unanimity that we would go on as long as he was comfortable," Richardson said. "Part of the reason was that we did the discussion literally ten feet in front of Barbaro. He's standing there, and he looks pretty damn good. He was pretty bright-eyed and looking at us. You can't turn around and kill a horse that looks that good if you love him that much."

Surgeons performed a hoof-wall resection, removing about 80 percent of his hoof wall because it wasn't connected to the coffin bone. Richardson treated Barbaro aggressively with pain medication. After the laminitis struck, his diagnosis was relegated to day to day: Barbaro had a very good night; he's stable at this time; his appetite is adequate today. But through it all, the horse kept his composure, kept the same attitude he had been known for from Sanborn Chase to Preakness Day to post-surgery.

"I've managed horses with laminitis that are basically unmanageable in terms of their pain," Richardson said. "We had a lot of things going for us with him that allowed us to deal with him."

The cast was changed on July 17, the incision examined, radiographs affirmative, new plates still set, fetlock fusion

By August, Barbaro is allowed some outdoor time

fine. The modified foot cast, to help with support, was changed. All this was done with Barbaro slightly sedated in a sling.

About ten days later Richardson changed the colt's cast and left hind foot bandage; everything looked like it was at least heading in the right direction. The infection in his right hind leg appeared to be under control.

By the time Matz and Prado packed up and went to Saratoga, Barbaro had started to turn another corner in his long recovery. His left hind hoof was showing evidence of regeneration, with the coronary band starting to exhibit downward growth. Still, all this was measured in millimeters, not inches. Because he was still bearing most of his weight in his right hind leg, the cast stayed on to support the pastern.

"I deal with horses that are hospitalized for a very long time, and even the best ones go through phases that they seem really dull. They go off their feed; they seem uninterested in their surroundings," Richardson said. "The one thing about Barbaro is that he's been a very, very tough horse in terms of his attitude. His appetite has been unbelievably good for a horse in his condition and the length of the hospitalization. He's been real tough."

On August 8 the cast that runs from just below the hock and encases the hoof was changed again, with Barbaro under general anesthesia. An old pro by now, Barbaro looked like Olympic gold medal winner Michael Phelps in the pool. Infection in the broken leg was gone, radiographs produced positive results, and the left hoof was dry, healthy, and showed excellent early growth along the coronary band.

And finally, outdoors; grass, sunshine, a fresh breeze. Barbaro went outside for brief periods to graze on a patch of grass near the intensive care unit.

By the end of August, he had had his cast changed again and was going out for a half-hour of grass. His blood work had returned to completely normal; his vital signs were strong; the sling was put away. Richardson continued to be awed by the horse.

"Barbaro's appetite and his attitude right now are phenomenal; he attacks his feed and when he goes out to graze, he acts like he thinks he could train," Richardson said at the time. "Right now, he is a surprisingly happy horse. He's gaining weight and has had his pain medications reduced without any effect on his well being. His strength and overall appearance have been improving since he became well enough to be walked outside each day."

Summer faded to fall and Barbaro gradually continued to improve. His right leg was getting stronger by the day, while his left hoof was growing fractionally — just as horses' hooves do. Barbaro was still on the long road, but the hazards of July had faded.

"For me, who is madly in love with this horse, it's increased my awe for him since his injury," Gretchen Jackson said in September. "He has just carried that look throughout, that 'I can deal.' He's just told us more than our brains have told us. We've just responded more to him and how he's been than going by the medical books."

The cast was changed again on October 9 and somehow, the once fateful reports started to sound almost mundane. Changed cast, radiographs good, no sign of infection, successful pool recovery, resting comfortably, enjoying grass. Hallelujah.

Barbaro loved his daily grazes. Sometimes, he'd go out

and just stand there, gazing across the New Bolton complex like he was looking for his barn at Fair Hill. Other times he'd scope out the two cows that were near his patch of grass, sniff and snort at them and wonder who they were. Other times he couldn't be bothered, he'd just eat. The neighboring private school's bus would drive past and the kids would yell out their window, "Baaaarbaro." He'd raise his head and stare at them.

Day after day, through laminitis that claimed most of his left hind foot — the good foot — through multiple surgeries and enough casts to keep a plaster company in business, Barbaro soldiered on, beating the odds so far.

Finally, on November 6, Richardson removed the cast on Barbaro's right leg for the final time, fitting Barbaro with a padded bandage with plastic and fiberglass splints. Put under general anesthesia, Barbaro woke up in his pool for the tenth time. Richardson and the team exhaled for the tenth time.

While Barbaro's right leg was able to bear full weight, the left hoof still needed several more months of growth before anybody knew its full structure or function, but for now it was on the right road.

As the year turned, Dr. Scott Morrison, head of the equine podiatry service at Rood and Riddle Equine Hospital in Lexington, Kentucky, examined Barbaro and did some minor work on his left hoof. Barbaro was comfortable and stable, his right leg solid, and his left hoof still under constant monitoring as it grew. If Barbaro survived his ordeal and one day moved to Kentucky, Morrison would be right in line to monitor the hoof.

And here we were, eight months after Barbaro's breakdown, still waiting to know if it was a miracle in equine science or a pipe dream stretched over an agonizing eternity.

"Like anybody else in this business, the only reason I'm in this business is because I love horses, and it's pretty easy to fall in love with a horse like him," Richardson said in early 2007. "He's got a lot of charisma, he's a great horse, and when you spend that much time with a horse, you're pretty involved."

Ask any horseman and he'll tell you he's shocked Barbaro made it that far. Numbers wise, Dr. Dreyfuss thought the colt had a 10 percent chance of making it when he left Pimlico; Dr. Richardson thought he had a less than 5 percent chance when he contracted laminitis in July. The others couldn't bear thinking about it.

No doctor wants to release a patient until fully cured, but Richardson felt it was time for Barbaro to go be a horse and get away from the stark atmosphere of an intensive care unit. Leading up to the Preakness, the horse thrived at the horse-friendly Fair Hill. He hadn't seen anything like it since he left for Pimlico the Friday morning before the Preakness. The horse needed to get around other horses, in a working barn where life would return to normal.

"It will be bittersweet," Richardson said as he imagined releasing his patient. "It will be bitter because I'll miss him, and I'm disappointed that he's not better than he is. For him to leave before he's perfect is upsetting. It will be sweet because at least we got him to the point where he's making a baby step towards his next career. We don't know if he'll get there. We don't know if he'll be able to cover a mare, but every effort will be made to get him comfortable enough to do it."

Matz always knew the horse was destined for something grand. First, he thought it was the Triple Crown; then, when he broke down, he thought, okay, it's to be a great

Dr. Dean Richardson and his famous patient

stallion. When the laminitis had him by the jugular, Matz didn't know what to think, even doubted his own instinct that the horse would do something far greater than win the Kentucky Derby. After eight months of rough seas, he was still unsure.

"I don't know what the answer is because it's still up in the air," Matz said. "By not being a racehorse but being a survivor, is that something bigger than if he won the Triple Crown? I don't know, but it's pretty special to have a horse like that."

In early January, the hero of this story walked with an obvious limp. He put his right hind leg down unnaturally but consistently and fairly steadily. With only one of three joints working, his right hind leg basically didn't bend from the hock to the hoof; it was more like a cane used for balance, but he walked. Yeah, he walked. He grazed. He nickered for the mares next door. He was a horse.

The public fell in love with Barbaro. They had good taste. Horses come in all shapes, sizes, attitudes, and personalities. It just so happens that Barbaro possessed the talent to reach stardom and the fortitude to overcome disaster while surrounded by a talented and dedicated group of caretakers who never gave up.

People love a hero — whether he beats death or dies trying. Barbaro died trying.

AUTHOR'S NOTE

As a lifelong horseman and the writer who lived on the periphery of this story, I wrote the book with one mindset — that Barbaro would make it. That was the only way I could look at it. As my deadline neared, it was rumored that Barbaro was preparing to leave New Bolton for a farm in Kentucky in hopes of standing stud in the future. We all hoped somewhere down the road we'd write another book about the peaceful life of Barbaro — living large and producing runners, in his birthplace, Lexington, Kentucky.

Two weeks after this book went to the printer, Barbaro was euthanized. The unflappable, undaunted Barbaro finally succumbed to complications from laminitis and it was over. Game called on January 29, 2007.

In the two-week span between the time I signed off on this book and Barbaro's death, people constantly asked me, "How's your book?" I said, "It will be a good read as long as he doesn't die between now and when it comes out."

I said it, almost matter of factly, until he died. Now, I'm not so sure of what kind of book this is. I'd like to think it is simply a tribute to a horse. A tribute to a horse who made us think, who made us cry, and who made us believe. — Sean

DELAWARE PARK - October 4, 2005 - Race 7

MAIDEN SPECIAL WEIGHT - For Thoroughbred Two Year Old
One Mile On The Turf **Track Record:** (Hanover Hollywood - 1:34.74 - August 3, 2002)

EQUIBASE C O M P A N Y

Purse: $40,000
Plus: $1,800 Starters Bonus
Available Money: $41,800
Value of Race: $41,800 1st $24,000, 2nd $8,000, 3rd $4,400, 4th $2,400, 5th $1,200, 6th $300, 7th $300, 8th $300, 9th $300, 10th $300, 11th $300
Weather: Showery **Track:** Firm
Off at: 3:32 **Start:** Good for all

Last Raced	Pgm	Horse Name (Jockey)	Wgt M/E	PP	Start	1/4	1/2	3/4	Str	Fin	Odds	Comments
---	10	Barbaro (Caraballo, Jose)	120 LA	9	3	$2^{1/2}$	2^2	1^1	1^4	$1^{8\ 1/2}$	7.50	hard to load,ridn out
10Sep05 ^{4}DEL^6	8	Jade's Revenge (Castillo, Jr., Heberto)	120 L b	7	7	$5^{1/2}$	5^{Head}	6^1	$3^{1/2}$	$2^{2\ 3/4}$	13.10	split h, second best
14Sep05 ^{6}LRL^{10}	3	Anasazi Moon (Carmouche, Kendrick)	120 L b	3	2	4^{Head}	4^{Head}	$3^{1/2}$	4^2	3^1	58.70	failed to gain
29Aug05 ^{7}DEL^5	4	Haajes (Pino, Mario)	120 LA b	4	4	$1^{1\ 1/2}$	$1^{1/2}$	2^2	2^2	4^{Neck}	11.20	drifted 1st turn,wknd
25Sep05 ^{7}DEL^8	7	Great Gusto (Rose, Jeremy)	120 LA b	6	9	7^1	7^{Head}	$5^{1/2}$	$5^{1/2}$	$5^{2\ 1/4}$	3.10	pushed out 1/4p
9Sep05 ^{4}BEL^6	2	Police Chief (Dominguez, Ramon)	120 LA	2	1	9^1	10^5	7^1	$6^{1/2}$	6^2	1.40*	passed tiring rivals
7Sep05 ^{2}DEL^7	12	Expressionism (Napravnik, A.)	114 LA b	11	5	3^1	3^1	$4^{1/2}$	7^2	$7^{1\ 1/4}$	109.20	drifted in,out,faded
24Sep05 ^{5}LRL^7	1	Dixie Demon (Bracho, Jesus)	120 LA b	1	11	10^1	8^1	$9^{1/2}$	$8^{1/2}$	$8^{1\ 1/2}$	22.60	ducked in st, no factr
24Sep05 ^{9}MTH^8	9	Lucky Straight (Umana, Juan)	120 L	8	8	11	11	11	$10^{1/2}$	9^{Nose}	39.00	trailed to mid stretch
25Sep05 ^{7}DEL^2	5	Obispo Street (Velazquez, Daniel)	120 L	5	10	$8^{1/2}$	$9^{1/2}$	$8^{1/2}$	9^3	10^3	5.00	showed little
25Sep05 ^{7}DEL^3	11	Nice Alex (Beitia, Alex)	120 --	10	6	6^2	$6^{1\ 1/2}$	10^4	11	11	34.60	stopped after half

Fractional Times: 23.71 47.68 1:12.21   **Final Time:** 1:35.87
Split Times: (23:97) (24:53) (23:66)

Winner: Barbaro, Dark Bay or Brown Colt, by Dynaformer out of La Ville Rouge, by Carson City. Foaled Apr 29, 2003 in Kentucky.
Breeder: Mr. & Mrs. M. Roy Jackson.   **Winning Owner:** Lael Stables

Scratched Horse(s): Magnum Power (Stewards), Tahoe Warrior (Also-Eligible)

Total WPS Pool: $106,112

Pgm	Horse	Win	Place	Show	Wager Type	Winning Numbers	Payoff	Pool
10	Barbaro	17.00	8.20	7.80	$2 Exacta	10-8	223.40	102,357
8	Jade's Revenge		12.40	6.40	$2 Trifecta	10-8-3	6,452.60	81,733
3	Anasazi Moon			18.40	$2 Daily Double	2-10	118.60	11,583
					$2 Pick 3	6-2-10 (3 correct)	1,066.00	7,818

Past Performance Running Line Preview

Pgm	Horse Name	Start	1/4	1/2	3/4	Str	Fin	E
1	Dixie Demon	11	10^8	$8^{5\ 1/4}$	9^7	$8^{11\ 1/2}$	8^{18}	58
2	Police Chief	1	9^7	$10^{6\ 3/4}$	$7^{5\ 1/2}$	6^9	$6^{14\ 3/4}$	63
3	Anasazi Moon	2	4^3	$4^{3\ 1/2}$	3^3	$4^{6\ 1/2}$	$3^{11\ 1/4}$	69
4	Haajes	4	$1^{1\ 1/2}$	$1^{1/2}$	2^1	2^4	$4^{12\ 1/4}$	67
5	Obispo Street	10	$8^{6\ 1/2}$	$9^{6\ 1/4}$	$8^{6\ 1/2}$	9^{12}	$10^{19\ 1/2}$	55
7	Great Gusto	9	$7^{5\ 1/2}$	$7^{5\ 1/4}$	5^4	$5^{8\ 1/2}$	$5^{12\ 1/2}$	67
8	Jade's Revenge	7	5^3	$5^{3\ 1/2}$	$6^{4\ 1/2}$	3^6	$2^{8\ 1/2}$	74
9	Lucky Straight	8	11^9	$11^{11\ 3/4}$	$11^{11\ 1/2}$	10^{15}	$9^{19\ 1/2}$	55
10	Barbaro	3	$2^{1\ 1/2}$	$2^{1/2}$	1^1	1^4	$1^{8\ 1/2}$	88
11	Nice Alex	6	$6^{3\ 1/2}$	$6^{3\ 3/4}$	$10^{7\ 1/2}$	$11^{15\ 1/2}$	$11^{22\ 1/2}$	50
12	Expressionism	5	3^2	$3^{2\ 1/2}$	$4^{3\ 1/2}$	$7^{9\ 1/2}$	$7^{16\ 3/4}$	60

Trainers: 10 - Matz, Michael; 8 - Motion, H.; 3 - Boniface, Kevin; 4 - Pino, Michael; 7 - Weaver, George; 2 - Klesaris, Steve; 12 - Rea, Michael; 1 - Tagg, Barclay; 9 - Wasiluk, Jr., Peter; 5 - Velazquez, Alfredo; 11 - Reyes, Alejandro

Owners: 10 - Lael Stables; 8 - Falls Church Racing Stable LLC; 3 - Flaxman Holdings, Ltd.; 4 - Shadwell Stable; 7 - Dogwood Stable; 2 - Puglisi Stables and Klesaris, Steve; 12 - Hardwicke Stable; 1 - Turf and Spa Stables; 9 - Bona Venture Stables; 5 - Anita Racing Stable; 11 - Reyes Segredo Family Stable;

Footnotes
BARBARO was hard to load in the gate, broke sharp to chase the leader outside, took over command after five furlongs then drew off through the final quarter under mild encouragement. JADE'S REVENGE raced boxed for six furlongs, split rivals out of the second turn and was clearly second best. ANASAZI MOON was forwardly placed but failed to gain after six furlongs. HAAJES drifted out through the first turn, set a moderate pace for five furlongs then weakened. GREAT GUSTO made an outside middle move then was pushed out passing the quarter pole, was forced to steady and failed to recover. POLICE CHIEF passed tiring rivals. EXPRESSIONISM stalked the pace outside, drifted in into the second turn then drifted out approaching the quarter pole and faded. DIXIE DEMON ducked in at the break then was no factor. LUCKY STRAIGHT trailed to mid stretch. OBISPO STREET showed little. NICE ALEX stopped after a half. The portable inner rail was set at zero feet.

LAUREL PARK - November 19, 2005 - Race 6
STAKES Laurel Futurity - For Thoroughbred Two Year Old
One And One Sixteenth Miles On The Turf **Track Record:** (Warning Glance - 1:39.35 - June 18, 1995)
Purse: $125,000 Guaranteed
Includes: $25,000 Other Sources
Available Money: $125,000
Value of Race: $125,000 1st $75,000, 2nd $25,000, 3rd $13,750, 4th $7,500, 5th $3,750
Weather: Clear **Track:** Firm
Off at: 2:44 **Start:** Good for all

Last Raced	Pgm	Horse Name (Jockey)	Wgt	M/E	PP	Start	1/4	1/2	3/4	Str	Fin	Odds	Comments
4Oct05 ^{7}DEL^1	7	Barbaro (Caraballo, Jose)	122	LA	6	4	$2^{1/2}$	2^1	2^2	$1^{3\,1/2}$	1^8	2.80	when ready 2wd,driving
28Oct05 ^{8}BEL^3	13	Diabolical (Dominguez, Ramon)	122	LA	13	8	5^1	4^1	$3^{1/2}$	2^6	2^2	5.70	4-3wd trip, willingly
4Nov05 ^{7}AQU^6	11	Exton (Rose, Jeremy)	117	L b	11	11	$12^{4\,1/2}$	$12^{4\,1/2}$	$9^{2\,1/2}$	$6^{1\,1/2}$	3^1	47.00	came 6wd,bothrd 3/16
20Oct05 ^{6}BEL^1	8	Rock Lobster (Coa, Eibar)	122	LA	7	10	9^1	8^{Head}	10^4	9^1	$4^{1/2}$	3.10	belated wide run
1Sep05 ^{7}SAL^3	6	Tent (IRE) (Douglas, Rene)	122	--	5	5	6^1	$6^{1/2}$	$6^{1\,1/2}$	7^{Head}	5^{Nose}	16.80	wide, checked 3/16
28Oct05 ^{9}KEE^2	4	Wedding Singer (Velazquez, John)	122	LA	3	12	11^{Head}	9^{Head}	7^2	$5^{1/2}$	$6^{1\,3/4}$	2.40*	pinched st,6wd,lug in
27Oct05 ^{4}LRL^4	5	Capo Dei Capi (Jurado, Enrique)	122	LA b	4	2	$1^{1\,1/2}$	$1^{1\,1/2}$	1^{Head}	$3^{1/2}$	$7^{1/2}$	49.40	pace ins, weakened
23Oct05 ^{8}DEL^2	2	Vegas Play (Garcia, Luis)	122	L b	2	3	3^1	3^{Head}	$4^{1/2}$	$4^{1/2}$	$8^{3/4}$	18.20	chased ins, gave way
15Oct05 ^{8}LRL^1	12	Creve Coeur (Prado, Edgar)	122	LA f	12	6	4^{Head}	5^1	$5^{2\,1/2}$	$8^{1/2}$	$9^{2\,1/2}$	10.20	btw far turn, gave way
2Nov05 ^{3}LRL^2	3	True Yield (Fogelsonger, Ryan)	117	LA b	1	1	8^1	10^1	8^{Head}	10^8	$10^{6\,1/2}$	31.20	ins early, no factor
25Sep05 ^{7}DEL^1	9	Potomac Manor (Pino, Mario)	122	LA b	9	13	13	13	13	11^2	11^3	135.90	lacked speed, no factr
9Oct05 ^{2}LRL^1	1A	Tactical Brush (Karamanos, Horacio)	122	LA b	8	7	10^{Head}	11^{Head}	$12^{3\,1/2}$	12^4	$12^{8\,1/2}$	18.20	checked nearing 1st
1Nov05 ^{9}DEL^1	10	Expressionism (Panell, Dyn)	122	LA b	10	9	7^{Head}	7^2	11^{Head}	13	13	198.80	3wd,checked 1st turn

Fractional Times: 23.03 46.87 1:10.83 1:34.34   **Final Time:** 1:40.17
Split Times: (23:84) (23:96) (23:51) (5:83)

Winner: Barbaro, Dark Bay or Brown Colt, by Dynaformer out of La Ville Rouge, by Carson City. Foaled Apr 29, 2003 in Kentucky.
Breeder: Mr. & Mrs. M. Roy Jackson.   **Winning Owner:** Lael Stables

Scratched Horse(s): Rockaby Bay (Trainer)

Total WPS Pool: $215,756

Pgm	Horse	Win	Place	Show	Wager Type	Winning Numbers	Payoff	Pool
7	Barbaro	7.60	4.60	6.40	$2 Exacta	7-13	51.60	175,527
13	Diabolical		5.80	5.20	$1 Superfecta	7-13-11-8	1,605.10	23,779
11	Exton			15.40	$2 Trifecta	7-13-11	1,353.00	113,136

Past Performance Running Line Preview

Pgm	Horse Name	Start	1/4	1/2	3/4	Str	Fin	E
1A	Tactical Brush	7	$10^{7\,1/4}$	$11^{8\,1/4}$	$12^{15\,3/4}$	12^{24}	$12^{26\,3/4}$	66
1	Vegas Play	3	3^2	$3^{2\,1/2}$	$4^{2\,1/2}$	4^{10}	$8^{13\,3/4}$	86
3	True Yield	1	$8^{5\,1/4}$	$10^{7\,1/4}$	8^9	10^{14}	10^{17}	81
4	Wedding Singer	12	$11^{7\,1/4}$	$9^{7\,1/4}$	7^7	$5^{10\,1/2}$	$6^{11\,1/2}$	90
5	Capo Dei Capi	2	$1^{1\,1/2}$	$1^{1\,1/2}$	1^{Head}	$3^{9\,1/2}$	$7^{13\,1/4}$	87
6	Tent (IRE)	5	6^4	$6^{4\,1/2}$	$6^{5\,1/2}$	$7^{12\,1/2}$	$5^{11\,1/2}$	90
7	Barbaro	4	$2^{1\,1/2}$	$2^{1\,1/2}$	2^{Head}	$1^{3\,1/2}$	1^8	108
8	Rock Lobster	10	$9^{6\,1/4}$	8^7	$10^{11\,3/4}$	9^{13}	4^{11}	91
9	Potomac Manor	13	13^{12}	13^{13}	$13^{19\,1/4}$	11^{22}	$11^{23\,1/2}$	71
10	Expressionism	9	7^5	7^5	$11^{15\,3/4}$	13^{28}	$13^{35\,1/4}$	53
11	Exton	11	$12^{7\,1/2}$	$12^{8\,1/2}$	$9^{9\,1/4}$	6^{11}	3^{10}	92
12	Creve Coeur	6	4^3	$5^{3\,1/2}$	5^3	$8^{12\,1/2}$	$9^{14\,1/2}$	85
13	Diabolical	8	5^3	$4^{2\,1/2}$	3^2	$2^{3\,1/2}$	2^8	95

Trainers: 7 - Matz, Michael; 13 - Klesaris, Steve; 11 - Schosberg, Richard; 8 - Dickinson, Michael; 6 - Cassidy, James; 4 - Pletcher, Todd; 5 - Tullock, Jr., Timothy; 1 - Delp, Grover; 12 - Motion, H.; 3 - Schoenthal, Phil; 9 - Blengs, Vincent; 1A - Delp, Grover; 10 - Rea, Michael

Owners: 7 - Lael Stables; 13 - Puglisi Stables and Klesaris, Steve; 11 - Brous Stable and Wachtel Stable; 8 - Flatbird Stable; 6 - Gould Family Trust; 4 - Dogwood Stable; 5 - Germania Farms, Inc.; 1 - Harry C. and Tom O. Meyerhoff LLC; 12 -Eugene F. Ford; 3 -Haywood Hyman, Jr; 9 -Wayne A. Harrison; 1a- Harry C. and Tom O. Meyerhoff LLC; 10 - Hardwicke Stable;

Footnotes
BARBARO stalked the pace off the rail, lodged a bid nearing the five sixteenth pole, drew clear near the quarter pole and drew off impressively under a steady drive. DIABOLICAL , four wide the first turn, continued well wide down the backstretch, advanced nearing the lane, finished willingly but was no match. EXTON settled in mid pack, circled six wide into the lane, was briefly steadied in upper stretch and finished willingly. ROCK LOBSTER , unhurried early, raced five to six wide in the lane and had some belated interest. TENT (IRE) , forwardly placed off the rail, came five wide for the drive, checked when impeded by WEDDING SINGER near the three sixteenths marker, then finished with some interest. WEDDING SINGER , bumped and pinched back at the break, moved up between rivals mid way down the backstretch, advanced six wide into the lane, lugged in near the three sixteenths marker then flattened out. CAPO DEI CAPI cleared early, set a brisk pace towards the inside, was collared after six furlongs then weakened nearing mid stretch. VEGAS PLAY chased the pace while saving ground and gave way. CREVE COEUR stalked the pace, raced between rivals into the far turn and gave way. TRUE YIELD saved ground early and failed to respond. POTOMAC MANOR lacked speed and failed to menace. TACTICAL BRUSH , checked nearing the first turn, raced wide into the backstretch and failed to recover. EXPRESSIONISM , three wide, checked around the first turn and dropped back.

CALDER RACE COURSE - January 1, 2006 - Race 11

STAKES Tropical Park Derby Grade 3 - For Thoroughbred Three Year Old
One And One Eighth Miles On The Turf **Track Record:** (The Vid - 1:44.99 - November 25, 1995)
Purse: $100,000 Guaranteed
Available Money: $100,000
Value of Race: $100,000 1st $60,000, 2nd $20,000, 3rd $11,000, 4th $6,000, 5th $3,000
Weather: Clear **Track:** Firm
Off at: 4:46 **Start:** Good for all except 12

Last Raced	Pgm	Horse Name (Jockey)	Wgt M/E	PP	Start	1/4	1/2	3/4	Str	Fin	Odds	Comments
19Nov05 6LRL1	5	Barbaro (Prado, Edgar)	119 L	4	2	2^1	2^1	2$^{1/2}$	2^{Head}	1$^{3\ 3/4}$	0.40*	ridden out
20Nov05 2CD3	3	Wise River (Blanc, Brice)	117 L	3	6	7$^{1/2}$	6^{Head}	6^{Head}	3^{Head}	2$^{3/4}$	18.60	saved grnd, no match
20Nov05 2CD1	1	Lewis Michael (Bridgmohan, Shaun)	119 L b	1	5	4^1	4^{Head}	4^1	4^2	3^{Nose}	6.70	no late response
10Dec05 11CRC3	10	Mr. Silver (Castro, Eddie)	119 L b	9	1	1$^{2\ 1/2}$	1$^{2\ 1/2}$	1$^{1\ 1/2}$	2^3	4$^{2\ 3/4}$	15.70	hedge, gave way
10Dec05 11CRC4	8	Can't Beat It (Bravo, Joe)	115 L b	7	7	6$^{1/2}$	5$^{1\ 1/2}$	5^{Head}	5^{Head}	5^1	28.10	3 wide, tired
23Nov05 7CD1	2	My Royal Man (Guidry, Mark)	117 L	2	10	11^{Head}	10$^{1\ 1/2}$	9$^{1/2}$	8^3	6$^{3/4}$	12.10	improved position
26Nov05 11CD7	7	International Cat (Velasquez, Cornelio)	117 L	6	11	8$^{1/2}$	9^1	8$^{1\ 1/2}$	7^{Head}	7^{Nose}	33.00	pinched back start
10Dec05 11CRC5	11	Allsmarts (Chavez, Jorge)	115 L b	10	4	3$^{1/2}$	3^1	3$^{1/2}$	6$^{1\ 1/2}$	8$^{2\ 1/4}$	114.60	3 wide, faltered
14Nov05 4CRC1	13	Manchu Prince (DeCarlo, Christopher)	115 L	12	8	9^{Head}	11^2	11$^{1/2}$	10$^{2\ 1/2}$	9$^{2\ 1/4}$	37.00	steadied 1st turn
19Nov05 6LRL6	12	Wedding Singer (Velazquez, John)	117 L b	11	12	10^1	8$^{1\ 1/2}$	7$^{1\ 1/2}$	9^1	10^1	10.90	hesitated start
26Nov05 7AQU8	6	Immersed in Gold (Castellano, Javier)	117 L	5	3	5$^{1/2}$	7^{Head}	10$^{2\ 1/2}$	11$^{3\ 1/2}$	11$^{2\ 3/4}$	41.40	through after 1/2
3Dec05 9CRC3	9	Rehoboth (Chapman, Kristi)	115 L b	8	9	12	12	12	12	12	103.90	outrun

Fractional Times: 23.32 47.89 1:12.20 1:35.39   **Final Time:** 1:46.65
Split Times: (24:57) (24:31) (23:19) (11:26)

Winner: Barbaro, Dark Bay or Brown Colt, by Dynaformer out of La Ville Rouge, by Carson City. Foaled Apr 29, 2003 in Kentucky.
Breeder: Mr. & Mrs. M. Roy Jackson.   **Winning Owner:** Lael Stables

Scratched Horse(s): Yankee Master (Trainer)

Total WPS Pool: $303,204

Pgm	Horse	Win	Place	Show	Wager Type	Winning Numbers	Payoff	Pool
5	Barbaro	2.80	2.80	2.20	$2 Exacta	5-3	26.80	264,598
3	Wise River		8.80	4.20	$2 Trifecta	5-3-1	69.60	211,739
1	Lewis Michael			3.20	$2 Superfecta	5-3-1-10	356.60	86,261

Past Performance Running Line Preview

Pgm	Horse Name	Start	1/4	1/2	3/4	Str	Fin	E
1	Lewis Michael	5	4^4	4$^{4\ 1/2}$	4$^{2\ 1/2}$	4$^{3\ 1/4}$	3$^{4\ 1/2}$	88
2	My Royal Man	10	11^8	10$^{8\ 3/4}$	9$^{6\ 3/4}$	8^7	6$^{8\ 1/4}$	82
3	Wise River	6	7^6	6^6	6$^{3\ 1/2}$	3^3	2$^{3\ 3/4}$	89
5	Barbaro	2	2$^{2\ 1/2}$	2$^{2\ 1/2}$	2$^{1\ 1/2}$	1^{Head}	1$^{3\ 3/4}$	95
6	Immersed in Gold	3	5^5	7$^{6\ 1/4}$	10$^{7\ 1/4}$	11$^{13\ 1/2}$	11$^{14\ 1/2}$	73
7	International Cat	11	8$^{6\ 1/2}$	9$^{7\ 3/4}$	8$^{5\ 1/4}$	7$^{6\ 3/4}$	7^9	81
8	Can't Beat It	7	6$^{5\ 1/2}$	5$^{4\ 1/2}$	5$^{3\ 1/2}$	5$^{5\ 1/4}$	5$^{7\ 1/4}$	84
9	Rehoboth	9	12$^{8\ 1/4}$	12$^{12\ 1/4}$	12$^{10\ 1/4}$	12^{17}	12$^{17\ 1/4}$	69
10	Mr. Silver	1	1$^{2\ 1/2}$	1$^{2\ 1/2}$	1$^{1\ 1/2}$	2^{Head}	4$^{4\ 1/2}$	88
11	Allsmarts	4	3$^{3\ 1/2}$	3$^{3\ 1/2}$	3^2	6$^{5\ 1/4}$	8^9	81
12	Wedding Singer	12	10^7	8$^{6\ 1/4}$	7$^{3\ 3/4}$	9^{10}	10$^{13\ 1/2}$	75
13	Manchu Prince	8	9^7	11$^{10\ 1/4}$	11$^{9\ 3/4}$	10^{11}	9$^{11\ 1/4}$	78

Trainers: 5 - Matz, Michael; 3 - Scott, Joan; 1 - Catalano, Wayne; 10 - Plesa, Jr., Edward; 8 - Wolfson, Martin; 2 - Romans, Dale; 7 - Abreu, Reynaldo; 11 - Brownlee, David; 13 - Pletcher, Todd; 12 - Pletcher, Todd; 6 - Kimmel, John; 9 - Gomez, Frank

Owners: 5 - Lael Stables; 3 - Pinebloom Stable; 1 - Frank Carl Calabrese; 10 - Thorobeam Farm and Mast, Henry; 8 - Live Oak Plantation; 2 - Whitestone Farm; 7 - Marylou Whitney Stables; 11 - J D Farms; 13 - Peachtree Stable; 12 - Dogwood Stable; 6 - Broman, Sr., Mary and Chester; 9 - J. Robert Harris, Jr.;

Footnotes

BARBARO stalked the pace, rallied to take over at the eighth pole and drew away under a hand ride. WISE RIVER rated off the pace, saved ground into the stretch, eased out and closed to gain the place while no match for the winner. LEWIS MICHAEL tracked the pace along the hedge, angled out for the drive and had no late response while edging MR. SILVER for the show. The latter, set the pace along the hedge into the stretch, responded when headed by the winner but gave way late. CAN'T BEAT IT raced in striking position three wide around the far turn and tired. MY ROYAL MAN unhurried early, saved ground and improved his position in the drive without threatening. INTERNATIONAL CAT failed to menace after being pinched back at the start. ALLSMARTS chased the pace three wide to nearing the stretch, then faltered. MANCHU PRINCE steadied in traffic soon after entering the first turn and was never a factor. WEDDING SINGER reserved after hesitating at the start, advanced four wide on the far turn to reach contention, then faded. IMMERSED IN GOLD was through after a half mile. REHOBOTH was outrun.

GULFSTREAM PARK - February 4, 2006 - Race 9

STAKES Holy Bull S. Grade 3 - For Thoroughbred Three Year Old
One And One Eighth Miles On The Dirt **Track Record:** (Brass Hat - 1:47.79 - February 4, 2006)
Purse: $150,000 Guaranteed
Available Money: $150,000
Value of Race: $150,000 1st $90,000, 2nd $30,000, 3rd $16,500, 4th $9,000, 5th $4,500
Weather: Showery **Track:** Sloppy (Sealed)
Off at: 4:50 **Start:** Good for all

Last Raced	Pgm	Horse Name (Jockey)	Wgt M/E	PP	Start	1/4	1/2	3/4	Str	Fin	Odds	Comments
1Jan06 [11]CRC[1]	5	Barbaro (Prado, Edgar)	122 L f	5	3	$2^{1\ 1/2}$	$2^{1/2}$	1^{Head}	$1^{1\ 1/2}$	$1^{3/4}$	1.60*	clear late, lasted
24Dec05 [7]CRC[1]	13	Great Point (Rose, Jeremy)	116 L b	12	9	12	12	$9^{1/2}$	6^4	$2^{2\ 1/2}$	25.00	traffic trn, late rush
7Jan06 [7]GP[3]	9	My Golden Song (Velazquez, John)	116 L	9	6	$6^{1\ 1/2}$	$6^{1/2}$	4^6	4^{Head}	$3^{1/2}$	11.20	5 wide, no late gain
26Nov05 [7]AQU[2]	8	Flashy Bull (Velasquez, Cornelio)	118 L	8	8	3^1	3^4	3^2	2^1	4^1	4.20	3 wide, gave way
7Jan06 [7]GP[2]	10	Itsallboutthechase (Guidry, Mark)	118 L b	10	10	9^4	9^8	$7^{1/2}$	$5^{1/2}$	$5^{3\ 3/4}$	7.50	couldn't sustain bid
7Jan06 [7]GP[1]	2	Doctor Decherd (Bridgmohan, Shaun)	120 L	2	1	1^1	$1^{1/2}$	2^1	3^1	$6^{3/4}$	9.30	inside, tired
15Jan06 [7]GP[2]	3	Sunriver (Bejarano, Rafael)	118 L	3	5	$4^{1/2}$	4^{Head}	$8^{1\ 1/2}$	7^6	$7^{3\ 3/4}$	7.80	3 wide, faltered
7Jan06 [8]AQU[5]	6	Fagan's Legacy (Castro, Eddie)	120 L	6	12	11^3	11^3	11^{Head}	8^{Head}	$8^{3/4}$	45.70	failed to menace
14Jan06 [9]LAD[5]	7	Saint Augustus (DeCarlo, Christopher)	120 L	7	7	7^{Head}	$8^{1/2}$	10^6	9^2	9^3	40.50	no factor
7Jan06 [7]GP[4]	1	Big Lover (Alvarado, Jr., Roberto)	116 L f	1	2	10^1	10^{Head}	12	$11^{1\ 1/2}$	10^{Head}	38.30	saved ground
19Dec05 [3]CRC[1]	4	Hemingway's Key (Castellano, Javier)	116 L	4	4	$5^{1\ 1/2}$	$5^{1/2}$	$5^{1/2}$	$10^{1/2}$	$11^{1\ 3/4}$	16.50	faded
26Nov05 [7]AQU[4]	12	Park Avenue Prince (Dominguez, Ramon)	118 L	11	11	8^1	7^2	$6^{1\ 1/2}$	12	12	32.50	saved ground

Fractional Times: 23.18 46.28 1:10.33 1:36.15   **Final Time:** 1:49.31
Split Times: (23:10) (24:05) (25:82) (13:16)

Winner: Barbaro, Dark Bay or Brown Colt, by Dynaformer out of La Ville Rouge, by Carson City. Foaled Apr 29, 2003 in Kentucky.
Breeder: Mr. & Mrs. M. Roy Jackson.   **Winning Owner:** Lael Stables

Scratched Horse(s): Barcola (Trainer), Rehoboth (Trainer)

Total WPS Pool: $706,104

Pgm	Horse	Win	Place	Show	Wager Type	Winning Numbers	Payoff	Pool
5	Barbaro	5.20	4.20	3.80	$1 Exacta	5-13	62.80	481,250
13	Great Point		14.40	9.40	$1 Trifecta	5-13-9	672.20	362,101
9	My Golden Song			6.40	$1 Superfecta	5-13-9-8	2,804.20	115,907
					$1 Pick 3	5-2-5 (3 correct)	52.00	84,129

Past Performance Running Line Preview

Pgm	Horse Name	Start	1/4	1/2	3/4	Str	Fin	E
1	Big Lover	2	10^{12}	$10^{16\ 1/2}$	$12^{19\ 3/4}$	$11^{16\ 3/4}$	$10^{16\ 3/4}$	95
2	Doctor Decherd	1	1^1	$1^{1/2}$	2^{Head}	$3^{2\ 1/2}$	$6^{8\ 1/2}$	99
3	Sunriver	5	$4^{3\ 1/2}$	4^5	$8^{11\ 1/2}$	7^8	$7^{9\ 1/4}$	99
4	Hemingway's Key	4	5^4	5^5	5^9	$10^{16\ 1/4}$	$11^{16\ 3/4}$	94
5	Barbaro	3	2^1	$2^{1/2}$	1^{Head}	$1^{1\ 1/2}$	$1^{3/4}$	104
6	Fagan's Legacy	12	11^{13}	$11^{16\ 3/4}$	$11^{19\ 1/2}$	8^{14}	8^{13}	97
7	Saint Augustus	7	7^7	8^8	$10^{13\ 1/2}$	$9^{14\ 1/4}$	$9^{13\ 3/4}$	96
8	Flashy Bull	8	$3^{2\ 1/2}$	3^1	3^1	$2^{1\ 1/2}$	$4^{3\ 3/4}$	102
9	My Golden Song	6	$6^{5\ 1/2}$	$6^{5\ 1/2}$	4^3	$4^{3\ 1/2}$	$3^{3\ 1/4}$	103
10	Itsallboutthechase	10	9^8	$9^{8\ 1/2}$	7^{11}	$5^{3\ 1/2}$	$5^{4\ 3/4}$	102
12	Park Avenue Prince	11	8^7	7^6	$6^{9\ 1/2}$	$12^{18\ 1/4}$	$12^{18\ 1/2}$	93
13	Great Point	9	12^{16}	$12^{19\ 3/4}$	9^{13}	6^4	$2^{3/4}$	104

Trainers: 5 - Matz, Michael; 13 - Zito, Nicholas; 9 - Pletcher, Todd; 8 - McLaughlin, Kiaran; 10 - Simms, Garry; 2 - Asmussen, Steven; 3 - Pletcher, Todd; 6 - Breen, Kelly; 7 - Pletcher, Todd; 1 - Salinas, Angel; 4 - Zito, Nicholas; 12 - Klesaris, Steve

Owners: 5 - Lael Stables; 13 - Robert V. LaPenta; 9 - Centaur Farms, Inc. (Heath); 8 - West Point Stable; 10 - Burr J. Travis; 2 - Mike McCarty; 3 - Jones, Aaron U. and Marie D.; 6 - Hall, George and Lori; 7 - Dogwood Stable; 1 - Michael H. Sherman; 4 - Kinsman Stable; 12 - Puglisi Stables and Klesaris, Steve;

Footnotes

BARBARO chased the pace, moved up to engage DOCTOR DECHARD midway of the far turn, drew clear from that rival approaching the eighth pole, increased his advantage approaching the sixteenth pole, then was all out to last over GREAT POINT. The latter, taken back and angled in to save ground racing into the first turn, was caught in traffic while advancing on the far turn, swung out for the stretch run, responded to pressure and closed with a late rush for the place. MY GOLDEN SONG rated off the pace, advanced into contention five wide on the far turn but couldn't gain late while up for the show. FLASHY BULL chased the pace three wide, made a run to reach the attending position in the stretch, then gave way. ITSALLBOUTTHECHASE allowed to settle, rallied four wide around the far turn to loom a threat in midstretch but couldn't sustain his bid. DOCTOR DECHERD quickly moved to the fore, made the pace along the inside, responded when headed by BARBARO on the far turn, stayed with that rival into the stretch, then tired. SUNRIVER well placed in behind the leaders, raced three wide on the far turn and faltered. FAGAN'S LEGACY failed to menace. SAINT AUGUSTUS was not a factor. BIG LOVER was outrun while saving ground. HEMINGWAY'S KEY reserved in striking position off the pace, raced in contention into the far turn, then faded. PARK AVENUE PRINCE saved ground into the far turn, then had nothing left for the drive.

EQUIBASE COMPANY

GULFSTREAM PARK - April 1, 2006 - Race 12
STAKES Florida Derby Grade 1 - For Thoroughbred Three Year Old
One And One Eighth Miles On The Dirt **Track Record:** (Brass Hat - 1:47.79 - February 4, 2006)
Purse: $1,000,000 Guaranteed
Available Money: $1,000,000
Value of Race: $1,000,000 1st $600,000, 2nd $190,000, 3rd $100,000, 4th $60,000, 5th $30,000, 6th $20,000
Weather: Clear **Track:** Fast
Off at: 5:43 **Start:** Good for all

Last Raced	Pgm	Horse Name (Jockey)	Wgt M/E	PP	Start	1/4	1/2	3/4	Str	Fin	Odds	Comments
4Feb06 ^{9}GP^1	10	Barbaro (Prado, Edgar)	122 L	10	6	2$^{1/2}$	2$^{1/2}$	2$^{1/2}$	2$^{2\,1/2}$	1$^{1/2}$	1.60*	bumped st, long drive
4Mar06 ^{7}GP^1	7	Sharp Humor (Guidry, Mark)	122 L	7	4	1$^{1\,1/2}$	1$^{1\,1/2}$	1$^{1/2}$	1^{Head}	2^3	6.40	rail trip, gamely
4Mar06 ^{3}GP^1	5	Sunriver (Velazquez, John)	122 L	5	3	7^{Head}	8$^{2\,1/2}$	5$^{1/2}$	4^{Head}	3$^{2\,1/4}$	4.30	steadied into 1st turn
11Mar06 ^{4}SA^1	11	Sam's Ace (Martinez, Felipe)	122 L	11	5	4$^{1/2}$	5^1	3$^{1\,1/2}$	3^{Head}	4$^{1/2}$	34.70	3 wide bid, gave way
18Mar06 ^{9}AQU^7	1	Hesanoldsalt (Castro, Eddie)	122 L b	1	2	3$^{1/2}$	4$^{1/2}$	4$^{1/2}$	5^4	5^4	39.90	hustled, tired
4Mar06 ^{3}GP^2	8	High Blues (Velasquez, Cornelio)	122 L f	8	9	9$^{1\,1/2}$	9$^{1/2}$	8^1	7^3	6$^{1/2}$	18.30	stdy st, bmpd 1st turn
4Mar06 ^{10}GP^2	2	Flashy Bull (Bejarano, Rafael)	122 L	2	1	5^{Head}	6$^{1/2}$	6^2	6^1	7$^{4\,1/4}$	4.00	steadied 1st turn
13Mar06 ^{4}GP^1	9	Charming Image (Maragh, Rajiv)	122 L b	9	11	11	11	11	11	8^{Neck}	92.00	bmpd, steadied start
26Feb06 ^{3}GP^1	3	Saint Augustus (DeCarlo, Christopher)	122 L	3	10	6^1	3^{Head}	9$^{1\,1/2}$	8^1	9$^{1\,1/4}$	25.50	rail, in tight early
26Feb06 ^{3}GP^2	4	Doc Cheney (Rose, Jeremy)	122 L	4	8	8$^{1\,1/2}$	7$^{1/2}$	7^1	9^1	10$^{1\,1/2}$	25.70	steadied twice 1st trn
4Mar06 ^{10}GP^5	6	Rehoboth (Castellano, Javier)	122 L b	6	7	10^3	10^2	10$^{2\,1/2}$	10$^{1\,1/2}$	11	9.70	bumped 1st turn

Fractional Times: 23.45 47.35 1:11.37 1:36.08 **Final Time:** 1:49.01
Split Times: (23:90) (24:02) (24:71) (12:93)

Winner: Barbaro, Dark Bay or Brown Colt, by Dynaformer out of La Ville Rouge, by Carson City. Foaled Apr 29, 2003 in Kentucky.
Breeder: Mr. & Mrs. M. Roy Jackson. **Winning Owner:** Lael Stables

Total WPS Pool: $1,563,853

Pgm	Horse	Win	Place	Show	Wager Type	Winning Numbers	Payoff	Pool
10	Barbaro	5.20	3.60	2.80	$1 Exacta	10-7	18.00	966,041
7	Sharp Humor		5.80	3.80	$1 Trifecta	10-7-5	59.60	842,703
5	Sunriver			3.60	$1 Superfecta	10-7-5-11	791.50	302,900
					$1 Pick 3	5-2-10 (3 correct)	21.40	120,373

Past Performance Running Line Preview

Pgm	Horse Name	Start	1/4	1/2	3/4	Str	Fin	E
1	Hesanoldsalt	2	3^2	4^2	4$^{2\,1/2}$	5$^{2\,3/4}$	5$^{6\,1/4}$	99
2	Flashy Bull	1	5^3	6$^{3\,1/2}$	6$^{3\,1/2}$	6$^{6\,3/4}$	7$^{10\,3/4}$	92
3	Saint Augustus	10	6^3	3^2	9$^{7\,1/2}$	8$^{10\,3/4}$	9$^{15\,1/4}$	85
4	Doc Cheney	8	8$^{4\,1/4}$	7^4	7$^{5\,1/2}$	9$^{11\,3/4}$	10$^{16\,1/2}$	83
5	Sunriver	3	7^4	8$^{4\,1/2}$	5^3	4$^{2\,3/4}$	3$^{3\,1/2}$	103
6	Rehoboth	7	10$^{7\,1/4}$	10$^{7\,1/2}$	10^9	10$^{12\,3/4}$	11^{18}	81
7	Sharp Humor	4	1$^{1\,1/2}$	1$^{1\,1/2}$	1$^{1/2}$	1^{Head}	2$^{1/2}$	107
8	High Blues	9	9$^{5\,3/4}$	9^7	8$^{6\,1/2}$	7$^{7\,3/4}$	6$^{10\,1/4}$	93
9	Charming Image	11	11$^{10\,1/4}$	11$^{9\,1/2}$	11$^{11\,1/2}$	11$^{14\,1/4}$	8^{15}	86
10	Barbaro	6	2$^{1\,1/2}$	2$^{1\,1/2}$	2$^{1/2}$	2^{Head}	1$^{1/2}$	108
11	Sam's Ace	5	4$^{2\,1/2}$	5$^{2\,1/2}$	3^1	3$^{2\,1/2}$	4$^{5\,3/4}$	99

Trainers: 10 - Matz, Michael; 7 - Romans, Dale; 5 - Pletcher, Todd; 11 - O'Neill, Doug; 1 - Zito, Nicholas; 8 - Paulus, David; 2 - McLaughlin, Kiaran; 9 - Pecoraro, Anthony; 3 - Pletcher, Todd; 4 - Zito, Nicholas; 6 - Gomez, Frank

Owners: 10 - Lael Stables; 7 - Purdedel Stable; 5 - Jones, Aaron U. and Marie D.; 11 - Reddam, J. Paul and Wellman, Aron; 1 - Live Oak Plantation; 8 - Dixiana Stables, Inc.; 2 - West Point Thoroughbreds LLC; 9 - Marc Wexler; 3 - Dogwood Stable; 4 - My Meadowview Farm; 6 - J. Robert Harris, Jr.;

Footnotes
BARBARO bobbled and bumped with CHARMING IMAGE at the start, moved up to prompt the pace outside SHARP HUMOR, made a run to reach near even terms for command midway of the far turn, then wore that rival down in a long drive to be up late. SHARP HUMOR quickly moved to fore, made the pace along the rail into the far turn, responded when challenged by BARBARO and continued on gamely while unable to resist that rival late. SUNRIVER steadied when caught in tight entering the first turn, eased out and advanced four wide around the far turn to loom a threat but had no late response. SAM'S ACE moved up quickly from the outside to gain position, stalked the pace three wide, made a run to reach the leaders on the far turn, then gave way in the drive. HESANOLDSALT hustled away from the gate, chased the pace off the rail into the stretch, then tired. HIGH BLUES reserved after being steadied from tight quarters at the start, bumped with REHOBOTH soon after entering the first turn and failed to menace. FLASHY BULL well placed in behind the leaders, steadied to avoid running up on those rivals leaving the first turn, remained in contention three wide into the far turn, then faltered. CHARMING IMAGE steadied when he bumped with BARBARO at the start, raced four wide around the far turn and was never a factor. SAINT AUGUSTUS was caught in tight along the rail soon after entering the first turn, raced in striking position along the inside into the far turn, then had nothing left. DOC CHENEY reserved off the pace after being steadied in tight quarters entering the first turn and again on the first turn, faded in the drive. REHOBOTH bumped with HIGH BLUES on the first turn and was outrun.

CHURCHILL DOWNS - May 6, 2006 - Race 10

STAKES Kentucky Derby Presented by Yum! Brands Grade 1 - For Thoroughbred Three Year Old
One And One Fourth Miles On The Dirt **Track Record:** (Secretariat - 1:59.40 - May 5, 1973)
Purse: $2,000,000 Guaranteed
Available Money: $2,213,200
Value of Race: $2,213,200 1st $1,453,200, 2nd $400,000, 3rd $200,000, 4th $80,000, 4th $80,000
Weather: Clear **Track:** Fast
Off at: 6:15 **Start:** Good for all except 8

Last Raced	Pgm	Horse Name (Jockey)	Wgt M/E	PP	1/4	1/2	3/4	1m	Str	Fin	Odds	Comments
1Apr06 ^{12}GP^1	8	Barbaro (Prado, Edgar)	126 L	8	5$^{1/2}$	4$^{1 1/2}$	4$^{1/2}$	1^3	1^4	1$^{6 1/2}$	6.10	stumble start,5w,drvng
15Apr06 ^{9}KEE^4	13	Bluegrass Cat (Dominguez, Ramon)	126 L	13	8$^{1/2}$	5$^{1/2}$	6$^{1/2}$	3^1	2$^{1/2}$	2^2	30.00	angled 4w lane,2nbest
15Apr06 ^{9}OP^2	2	Steppenwolfer (Albarado, Robby)	126 L	2	18$^{1/2}$	13^{Head}	11$^{1/2}$	6^{Head}	5^1	3^1	16.30	bmp start,forced in,6w
8Apr06 ^{8}AQU^2	1	DH-Jazil (Jara, Fernando)	126 L c	1	20	20	19$^{1/2}$	17^2	6^1	4$^{1/2}$	24.20	swerve in start,empty
8Apr06 ^{6}SA^1	18	DH-Brother Derek (Solis, Alex)	126 L	18	9$^{1 1/2}$	9$^{1/2}$	14$^{1/2}$	10^{Head}	7$^{1/2}$	4$^{1/2}$	7.70	steadied twice,9w
22Apr06 ^{9}KEE^1	6	Showing Up (Velasquez, Cornelio)	126 L	6	4^{Head}	3^{Head}	3^{Head}	2^{Head}	3$^{1 1/2}$	6^3	26.20	bobble,bmp strt,4w bid
8Apr06 ^{7}HAW^1	11	Sweetnorthernsaint (Desormeaux, Kent)	126 L b	11	12^1	11^1	5$^{1/2}$	4^{Head}	4^{Head}	7^1	5.50*	bmp strt,steadied,tire
8Apr06 ^{8}AQU^6	14	Deputy Glitters (Lezcano, Jose)	126 L	14	13^1	15$^{1/2}$	16$^{1/2}$	9^1	10^1	8$^{1 1/4}$	60.60	11w lane,bmp 1/8p
8Apr06 ^{6}SA^2	5	Point Determined (Bejarano, Rafael)	126 L b	5	11$^{1/2}$	10^{Head}	7$^{1/2}$	7^{Head}	8$^{1/2}$	9^{Head}	9.40	5w bid,bmp 1/8p,tired
15Apr06 ^{9}KEE^6	15	Seaside Retreat (Husbands, Patrick)	126 L	15	7^{Head}	7$^{1 1/2}$	10$^{1/2}$	15^{Head}	9^{Head}	10$^{4 1/2}$	52.50	6w, bmp 1/8p,tired
15Apr06 ^{9}KEE^2	19	Storm Treasure (Flores, David)	126 L	19	19$^{2 1/2}$	18^2	13^{Head}	12^{Head}	11$^{1/2}$	11$^{1 3/4}$	51.90	between,empty in lane
15Apr06 ^{9}OP^1	17	Lawyer Ron (McKee, John)	126 L	17	6$^{1/2}$	8$^{1/2}$	9$^{1/2}$	8$^{1/2}$	12$^{1 1/2}$	12$^{1 1/2}$	10.20	steadied 3/4p,tired,6w
8Apr06 ^{7}HAW^3	16	Cause to Believe (Baze, Russell)	126 L	16	15$^{1/2}$	19^2	20	18^4	17^2	13^3	25.90	failed to menace
1Apr06 ^{12}GP^7	20	Flashy Bull (Smith, Mike)	126 L c	20	16^1	17^{Head}	17^1	14$^{1/2}$	15^1	14$^{2 1/2}$	43.00	broke awkward,wide
15Apr06 ^{9}OP^3	12	Private Vow (Bridgmohan, Shaun)	126 L	12	17^1	16$^{1/2}$	12$^{1/2}$	11$^{1/2}$	14$^{1 1/2}$	15$^{2 3/4}$	40.50	slw start,bmp,steady
15Apr06 ^{9}KEE^1	4	Sinister Minister (Espinoza, Victor)	126 L b	4	2$^{1 1/2}$	2^2	2$^{1 1/2}$	5^1	13$^{1 1/2}$	16$^{1 1/2}$	9.70	pressed,led,faded
8Apr06 ^{8}AQU^1	7	Bob and John (Gomez, Garrett)	126 L b	7	14$^{1/2}$	12^1	8^{Head}	16$^{1/2}$	16$^{1/2}$	17^{Neck}	12.90	bmp start,steadied
8Apr06 ^{6}SA^3	10	A. P. Warrior (Nakatani, Corey)	126 L	10	10$^{1/2}$	14^1	18$^{1/2}$	19^5	19^5	18$^{1 1/2}$	14.10	came out bmp start
1Apr06 ^{12}GP^2	9	Sharp Humor (Guidry, Mark)	126 L	9	3$^{1 1/2}$	6^{Head}	15$^{1 1/2}$	20	20	19$^{7 1/2}$	30.10	faded,bore out 3/8p
8Apr06 ^{8}AQU^3	3	Keyed Entry (Valenzuela, Patrick)	126 L	3	1^{Head}	1^2	1$^{1 1/2}$	13^{Head}	18$^{2 1/2}$	20	28.80	duck in bmp strt,faded

Fractional Times: 22.63 46.07 1:10.88 1:37.02   **Final Time:** 2:01.36
Split Times: (23:44) (24:81) (26:14) (24:34)

Winner: Barbaro, Dark Bay or Brown Colt, by Dynaformer out of La Ville Rouge, by Carson City. Foaled Apr 29, 2003 in Kentucky.
Breeder: Mr. & Mrs. M. Roy Jackson.   **Winning Owner:** Lael Stables

Dead Heats: 4th place - # 1 Jazil
                      4th place - #18 Brother Derek

Total WPS Pool: $49,682,267

Pgm	Horse	Win	Place	Show	Wager Type	Winning Numbers	Payoff	Pool
8	Barbaro	14.20	8.00	6.00	$2 Exacta	8-13	587.00	23,071,712
13	Bluegrass Cat		28.40	15.40	$2 Trifecta	8-13-2	11,418.40	27,062,557
2	Steppenwolfer			7.80	$2 Superfecta	8-13-2-1	84,860.40	8,776,694
					$2 Superfecta	8-13-2-18	59,839.00	0

Trainers: 8 - Matz, Michael; 13 - Pletcher, Todd; 2 - Peitz, Daniel; 1 - McLaughlin, Kiaran; 18 - Hendricks, Dan; 6 - Tagg, Barclay; 11 - Trombetta, Michael; 14 - Albertrani, Thomas; 5 - Baffert, Bob; 15 - Casse, Mark; 19 - Asmussen, Steven; 17 - Holthus, Robert; 16 - Hollendorfer, Jerry; 20 - McLaughlin, Kiaran; 12 - Asmussen, Steven; 4 - Baffert, Bob; 7 - Baffert, Bob; 10 - Shirreffs, John; 9 - Romans, Dale; 3 - Pletcher, Todd

Owners: 8 - Lael Stables; 13 - WinStar Farm LLC; 2 - Low, Lawana L. and Robert E.; 1 - Shadwell Stable; 18 - Cecil N. Peacock; 6 - Lael Stables; 11 - Balsamo, Joseph J. and Theos, Ted; 5 - Joseph Lacombe Stable, Inc.; 15 - Robert and Beverly Lewis Trust; 15 - William S. Farish, Jr.; 19 - Mike McCarty; 17 - Estate of James T. Hines, Jr.; 16 - Abruzzo, Peter and Peter Redekop B. C. Ltd; 20 - West Point Thoroughbreds LLC; 12 - Mike McCarty; 4 - Lanni Family Trust, Mercedes Stable, LLC and Schiappa, Bernard C.; 7 - Stonerside Stable; 10 - Stan E. Fulton; 9 - Purdedel Stable and WinStar Farm LLC, Lessee; 3 - Starlight Stable and Lucarelli, Donald J.;

Footnotes
BARBARO stumbled at the start, came up running and leaned in soon after bumping with BOB AND JOHN placing him in tight, raced under light restraint while between horses early, continued three wide around the first turn then swung five to six wide into the backstretch, raced to the leaders under his own power midway on the far turn, reached the front at the five-sixteenths pole, accelerated quickly to a clear advantage approaching the stretch while angling near the inside, then drew off under strong hand urging as much the best. BLUEGRASS CAT, never far back, maneuvered nicely between foes to reach the rail entering the first turn, followed BARBARO while just inside that one on the backstretch, angled outside the winner nearing the final quarter, then couldn't menace at the end while clearly second best. STEPPENWOLFER, bumped after the start by KEYED ENTRY and forced in, saved ground in hand, rallied between horses three or four wide on the far turn, lacked room at the five-sixteenths pole, worked his way out six wide when straightened into the stretch to make his run, loomed a threat through the upper stretch, then failed to sustain his bid while drifting out slightly. JAZIL swerved in at the start, was unhurried while outrun for six furlongs, continued to save ground while rallying along the rail on the far turn, angled out between foes four wide when entering the upper stretch to make a serious bid but failed to sustain his effort while dead heating with BROTHER DEREK for fourth. BROTHER DEREK worked his way in six wide by the first turn, moved out wider when the field bunched nearing the end of the backstretch where he was steadied twice, fanned out nine abreast when making a run into the upper stretch, but came up empty while finishing evenly with JAZIL for fourth. SHOWING UP bobbled at the break, came out bumping with BOB AND JOHN, gained a forward position near the inside, went along under careful handling, raced between foes four wide nearing the final quarter, was just off the winner briefly when entering the stretch and flattened out in the drive. SWEETNORTHERNSAINT, steadied when bumped at the start by A.P. WARRIOR and forced out on PRIVATE VOW, was steadied again under the wire the first time in tight quarters, worked his way between foes around the first turn, angled inside on the backstretch, boldly came through close quarters along the rail at the five-sixteenths pole, but faltered when straightened for the drive. DEPUTY GLITTERS, outrun five wide into the backstretch, inched forward around the far turn, came out eleven wide for the drive, leaned in and bumped SEASIDE REATREAT at the furlong grounds, then lacked a further response. POINT DETERMINED, bobbled lightly at the start, was well placed near the inside from the outset, moved between horses five wide into the lane, came out and bumped with SEASIDE RETREAT at the eighth pole and was finished. SEASIDE RETREAT, unhurried and six wide, reached striking distance on the far turn, came out wider entering the stretch, was bumped from both sides at the eighth pole and had no further account. STORM TREASURE, steadied behind horses nearing the first turn, made a mild move between rivals approaching the final quarter but failed to continue. LAWYER RON, well placed early, raced between foes around the first turn, was steadied entering the backstretch, continued within striking distance into the stretch and tired. CAUSE TO BELIEVE never reached contention. FLASHY BULL broke awkwardly and raced wide most of the way. PRIVATE VOW, sluggish to start, was bumped soon after by SWEETNORTHERNSAIT and steadied, then never was a factor. SINISTER MINISTER vied for the lead soon after start while battling outside of KEYED ENTRY, surrendered the advantage to that one just before the opening quarter expired, tracked KEYED ENTRY to the far turn, briefly gained the lead between calls approaching the stretch, lost it to the winner after several strides and faded. BOB AND JOHN, bumped at the start by SHOWING UP, then steadied soon after and bumped again when BARBARO leaned in, was finished after seven furlongs. A. P. WARRIOR came out at the start bumping SWEETNORTHERNSAINT, then was finished early. SHARP HUMOR came out after the start bumping A.P. WARRIOR, faded after a half, bore out midway on the second turn and wasn't abused in the drive. KEYED ENTRY leaned in at the start bumping STEPPENWOLFER, went up inside SINISTER MINISTER to fight for the lead, gained a slight edge after going a quarter, was clear on the first turn, showed the way to the far turn and gave way readily after seven furlongs.

PIMLICO - May 20, 2006 - Race 12
STAKES Preakness S. Grade 1 - For Thoroughbred Three Year Old
One And Three Sixteenth Miles On The Dirt **Track Record:** (Farma Way - 1:52.55 - May 11, 1991)
Purse: $1,000,000 Guaranteed
Available Money: $1,000,000
Value of Race: $1,000,000 1st $600,000, 2nd $200,000, 3rd $110,000, 4th $60,000, 5th $30,000
Weather: Clear **Track:** Fast
Off at: 6:19 **Start:** Good for all

Last Raced	Pgm	Horse Name (Jockey)	Wgt M/E	PP	Start	1/4	1/2	3/4	Str	Fin	Odds	Comments
29Apr06 ^{3}AQU^1	8	Bernardini (Castellano, Javier)	126 L	8	5	3^1	4^2	4^4	1$^{3\,1/2}$	1$^{5\,1/4}$	12.90	lug in, steady urging
6May06 ^{10}CD^7	7	Sweetnothernsaint (Desormeaux, Kent)	126 LA b	7	2	2$^{1\,1/2}$	3$^{1/2}$	2$^{1\,1/2}$	2^6	2^6	8.40	2-3w,led 1/4,shied in
22Apr06 ^{9}KEE^8	3	Hemingway's Key (Rose, Jeremy)	126 LA c	3	7	7$^{1\,1/2}$	7$^{1/2}$	7$^{1/2}$	4^4	3^4	29.40	rail,angled 3/16
6May06 ^{10}CD^4	5	Brother Derek (Solis, Alex)	126 L	5	9	5^4	2^{Head}	3^2	3$^{1\,1/2}$	4^7	3.20	std'd,checkd early,4wd
22Apr06 ^{9}KEE^4	4	Greeley's Legacy (Migliore, Richard)	126 L bf	4	3	8	8	6^1	6^1	5^{Neck}	34.90	steadied early, wide
8Apr06 ^{8}AQU^5	2	Platinum Couple (Espinoza, Jose)	126 L f	2	4	6^3	6$^{2\,1/2}$	8	8	6$^{3\,1/2}$	33.20	finished after 3/4's
22Apr06 ^{9}KEE^2	1	Like Now (Gomez, Garrett)	126 LA	1	1	1$^{1/2}$	1^1	1$^{1/2}$	5^2	7$^{2\,1/4}$	17.40	pressured ins,tired
25Apr06 ^{8}DEL^1	9	Diabolical (Dominguez, Ramon)	126 LA	9	6	4$^{1\,1/2}$	5^5	5^4	7^1	8	26.00	chased inside, tired
6May06 ^{10}CD^1	6	Barbaro (Prado, Edgar)	126 LA	6	8	---	---	---	---	---	0.50*	broke down

Fractional Times: 23.21 46.69 1:10.24 1:35.73   **Final Time:** 1:54.65
Split Times: (23:48) (23:55) (25:49) (18:92)

Winner: Bernardini, Bay Colt, by A.P. Indy out of Cara Rafaela, by Quiet American. Foaled Mar 23, 2003 in Kentucky.
Breeder: Darley. **Winning Owner:** Darley Stable

Total WPS Pool: $21,156,656

Pgm	Horse	Win	Place	Show	Wager Type	Winning Numbers	Payoff	Pool
8	Bernardini	27.80	9.40	5.80	$2 Pick 3	1-1/4-8 (3 correct)	446.20	434,873
7	Sweetnothernsaint		7.80	5.00	$2 Pick 4	4-1-1/4-8 (4 correct)	1,620.80	1,462,048
3	Hemingway's Key			8.00	$2 Daily Double	1-8	66.20	419,627
					$2 Daily Double	SPECIAL/PREAKNESS 4-8	121.00	470,883
					$2 Exacta	8-7	171.60	12,186,518
					$1 Superfecta	8-7-3-5	11,151.20	6,488,237
					$2 Trifecta	8-7-3	3,912.80	15,631,720

Past Performance Running Line Preview

Pgm	Horse Name	Start	1/4	1/2	3/4	Str	Fin	E
1	Like Now	1	1$^{1/2}$	1^1	1$^{1/2}$	5^{15}	7^{26}	91
2	Platinum Couple	4	6$^{8\,1/2}$	6$^{8\,1/2}$	8$^{13\,1/2}$	8^{19}	6$^{22\,1/2}$	96
3	Hemingway's Key	7	7$^{11\,1/2}$	7^{11}	7^{13}	4^{11}	3$^{11\,1/4}$	112
4	Greeley's Legacy	3	8^{13}	8$^{11\,1/2}$	6^{12}	6^{17}	5$^{22\,1/4}$	96
5	Brother Derek	9	5$^{4\,1/2}$	2^1	3^2	3$^{9\,1/2}$	4$^{15\,1/4}$	106
6	Barbaro	8	---	---	---	---	---	---
7	Sweetnothernsaint	2	2$^{1/2}$	3^1	2$^{1/2}$	2$^{3\,1/2}$	2$^{5\,1/4}$	120
8	Bernardini	5	3^2	4$^{1\,1/2}$	4^4	1$^{3\,1/2}$	1$^{5\,1/4}$	127
9	Diabolical	6	4^3	5$^{3\,1/2}$	5^8	7^{18}	8$^{28\,1/4}$	88

Trainers: 8 - Albertrani, Thomas; 7 - Trombetta, Michael; 3 - Zito, Nicholas; 5 - Hendricks, Dan; 4 - Weaver, George; 2 - Lostritto, Joseph; 1 - McLaughlin, Kiaran; 9 - Klesaris, Steve; 6 - Matz, Michael

Owners: 8 - Darley Stable; 7 - Balsamo, Joseph J. and Theos, Ted; 3 - Kinsman Stable; 5 -Cecil N. Peacock; 4 -Donald F. Flanagan; 2 - Team Tristar Stable; 1 -John J. Dillon; 9 - Puglisi Stables and Klesaris, Steve; 6 - Lael Stables;

Footnotes
BERNARDINI was patiently rated three to four wide between rivals into the backstretch, took a firm hold when BROTHER DEREK made his move midway down the backstretch, angled in leaving the far turn, swung back out four wide approaching the quarter pole, surged to command in upper stretch, lugged in briefly nearing the eighth pole, responding to strong left handed urging, opened a clear advantage in midstretch and drew off through the final sixteenth while under a vigorous hand ride in the final seventy yards. SWEETNORTHERNSAINT prompted the pace two to three wide, moved to near even terms for the lead leaving the far turn, opened a clear lead leaving the quarter pole, shied inward once headed at the three sixteenths pole, drifted out in mid stretch and was clearly best of the rest. HEMINGWAY'S KEY was outrun early, saved ground to the quarter pole, angled out in upper stretch, drifted out briefly near the furlong marker then finished willingly once straightened to gain a share. BROTHER DEREK broke a step slow then steadied soon after, checked off the heels of BARBARO under the wire the first time, altered course to the four path, rushed up entering the backstretch, chased the leaders while continuing four wide into the far turn then faded from the quarter pole. GREELEY'S LEGACY was steadied early, raced wide and failed to menace. PLATINUM COUPLE flashed only brief speed and dropped back after six furlongs. LIKE NOW was away alertly, sprinted clear nearing the first turn, set a pressured pace towards the inside leaving the backstretch, dueled around the final turn, was headed leaving the five-sixteenths marker then tired in upper stretch. DIABOLICAL was angled to the rail nearing the first turn, chased the leaders for six furlongs then faltered. BARBARO broke through the gate pre race then was pulled up after breaking down in his right hind when nearing the wire the first time.

				ROYAL CHARGER, 1942
			TURN-TO, 1951	SOURCE SUCREE, 1940
		HAIL TO REASON, 1958		BLUE SWORDS, 1940
	ROBERTO, 1969		NOTHIRDCHANCE, 1948	GALLA COLORS, 1943
			NASHUA, 1952	NASRULLAH, 1940
		BRAMALEA, 1959		SEGULA, 1942
			RARELEA, 1949	BULL LEA, 1935
DYNAFORMER, 1985				BLEEBOK, 1941
			RIBOT, 1952	TENERANI, 1944
		HIS MAJESTY, 1968		ROMANELLA, 1943
			FLOWER BOWL, 1952	ALIBHAI, 1938
	ANDOVER WAY, 1978			FLOWER BED, 1946
			OLYMPIA, 1946	HELIOPOLIS, 1936
		ON THE TRAIL, 1964		MISS DOLPHIN, 1934
			GOLDEN TRAIL, 1958	HASTY ROAD, 1951
BARBARO				SUNNY VALE, 1946
			RAISE A NATIVE, 1961	NATIVE DANCER, 1950
		MR. PROSPECTOR, 1970		RAISE YOU, 1946
			GOLD DIGGER, 1962	NASHUA, 1952
	CARSON CITY, 1987			SEQUENCE, 1946
			BLUSHING GROOM, 1974	RED GOD, 1954
		BLUSHING PROMISE, 1982		RUNAWAY BRIDE, 1962
			SUMMERTIME PROMISE, 1972	NIJINSKY II, 1967
LA VILLE ROUGE, 1996				PRIDES PROMISE, 1966
			ROUND TABLE, 1954	PRINCEQUILLO, 1940
		KING'S BISHOP, 1969		KNIGHT'S DAUGHTER, 1941
			SPEARFISH, 1963	FLEET NASRULLAH, 1955
	LA REINE ROUGE, 1978			ALABAMA GAL, 1957
			NEARCTIC, 1954	NEARCO, 1935
		SILVER BETSY, 1971		LADY ANGELA, 1944
			SILVER ABBEY, 1958	DJEDDAH, 1945
				GOLDARETTE, 1952

**BARBARO, DARK BAY OR BROWN COLT, FOALED APRIL 29, 2003
BRED IN KENTUCKY BY MR. AND MRS. M. ROY JACKSON**

187

COVER PHOTO: Barbara D. Livingston

BACK COVER: Barbara D. Livingston; Skip Dickstein

BARBARA D. LIVINGSTON: 5, 7, 10, 24, 39, 40, 43, 44, 46, 66, 68, 69, 70, 72, 73, 74, 76, 80, 82, 84, 96, 105, 106, 108, 110, 115, 116, 119, 126, 127, 138, 139, 144, 146, 150, 168, 169

BENOIT & ASSOCIATES: 13, 36

CHERYL MANISTA: 14

TONY LEONARD: 16

ANNE M. EBERHARDT: 18, 64

SANDY SANBORN: 19

LOUISE J. REINAGEL: 20, 21

DOUG ENGLE: 22

USET: 27

KIT HOUGHTON: 28

SHAWN HAMILTON: 30

AP WORLDWIDE: 31, 157

BILL DENVER/EQUI-PHOTO: 32, 62

SKIP DICKSTEIN: 37, 94, 97, 100, 104, 114, 137, 142

LYDIA A. WILLIAMS: 38, 49, 113, 170

MARY LYONS: 48

JIM MCCUE/MARYLAND JOCKEY CLUB: 50

JIM LISA: 52, 55

MATT DEAN/EQUI-PHOTO: 56, 60

RYAN MCALINDEN/EQUI-PHOTO: 58, 61

JEFFREY SNYDER: 59, 120

ALEXANDER BARKOFF: 86, 101, 104

DAVE SNYDER: 88, 133

DAVE BLACK: 90, 91

MIKE CORRADO: 92, 103

LUCAS GILMAN: 98

MAX MORSE: 102

ALYSSE JACOBS: 122

RICK SAMUELS: 125, 128, 141

BILL AUTH: 130, 132, 134, 136, 140, 143

DAVE HARMON: 137

AP IMAGES/MATT ROURKE: 154, 160

HO/REUTERS/CORBIS: 150

CORBIS/SABINA LOUISE PIERCE: 167

AP IMAGES/JOSEPH KACZMAREK: 162

AP IMAGES/GEORGE WIDMAN: 164, 172, 175, 178

STEPHANIE CHURCH: 191

PHOTO CREDITS

ABOUT THE AUTHOR

Sean Clancy, a critically acclaimed author and former champion jockey, has had a lifelong association with horses. His father, Joe Clancy Sr., trained flat and steeplechase horses and instilled in sons Sean and Joe Jr. a love of racing.

Sean Clancy had quite a career as a jockey, riding steeplechase races professionally for 13 years. He won a total of 152 races and a national championship in 1998. He was the 10th highest winner of all time upon his retirement in 2000.

Clancy is the author of *Saratoga Days* and co-author of *The Best of the Saratoga Special*. He also has written for *Daily Racing Form*, *The Blood-Horse*, *Mid-Atlantic Thoroughbred*, and *Newsweek* among others.

Clancy is editor/publisher of ST Publishing, based in Fair Hill, Maryland. ST Publishing produces *The Saratoga Special*, *Steeplechase/Eventing Times*, *The Special at Keeneland*, *Thoroughbred Racing Calendar*, and other projects.

Clancy's connections to Barbaro are many. He grew up in Unionville, Pennsylvania, home of Barbaro's owners, Roy and Gretchen Jackson; Barbaro's trainer Michael Matz; and Barbaro's temporary home, University of Pennsylvania's New Bolton Center. Clancy lives in Landenberg, Pennsylvania, hometown of Barbaro's primary veterinarian, Dr. Dean Richardson, and his office is in Fair Hill, Maryland, Barbaro's training grounds.

SEAN CLANCY